Eati

in Birmingham
and the Midlands

by

Alison Davison

of The Birmingham Post

Astoria Publishing Ltd

All the restaurants and pubs in this book are considered to be of a sufficiently decent standard to warrant a visit. Particularly good places are marked with one ★; outstandingly good ones get 2★★. The ratings were decided after independent inspections. No establishment pays to get in and no advertising is accepted.

All prices and menu information were correct at the time of going to press. Details in the margins on opening times, vegetarian options etc were provided by the restaurants and pubs themselves. Mention in the margin of free range, organic or local produce means partial or occasional use – not exclusive use.

KEY

All establishments have a non-smoking section and play background music unless otherwise stated.

 The restaurant is smoking throughout

 There is a non-smoking dining room (although there may be a bar area for smokers)

 Children's portions or a children's menu are available

 No background music

 Outdoor dining available

 Car parking available

 The venue has an outstanding wine list

V – number of vegetarian options at main course

A/C – air-conditioned

CC – credit cards

L – lunch

D – dinner

Alc – À la carte

Organic/free range/local produce – some of these items will be used but not exclusively.

FOREWORD
by Raymond Blanc

The greatness of a city is usually measured by its architecture, museums, universities, concert halls, commerce, shopping . . . all of these are definitive indications of a city's status.

Today, we must add one more important measurement: restaurants! Yes, a healthy vibrant restaurant life is a sure yardstick to measure the sophistication of a city. More and more, the table is being established as a powerful medium to celebrate life, friendship, ourselves and, of course, the beautiful food.

Birmingham has changed beyond recognition. Huge chunks of the city are being ground down and magically reinvented.

Birmingham is on a mission. Rarely have I seen so much energy, creativity and resolve channelled into one city. Restaurant life in Birmingham and the Midlands is buzzing; the choice is enormous and the food very good.

Tables are spilling out onto the pavements, squares and on the canalsides - one hears laughter and the clinking of wine glasses.

We at Le Petit Blanc are very proud to be part of this great adventure.

At last, here is a restaurant guide to acknowledge the variety and quality of the eating out scene in Birmingham and the Midlands.

I hope you will be visiting all of these places. Naturally, we look forward to welcoming you at Le Petit Blanc.

Raymond Blanc

INTRODUCTION

Since April 1997, I have eaten my way around
Birmingham and a large chunk of the Midlands on
behalf of The Birmingham Post, whose Wednesday
eating out guide I edit.
The experiences have ranged from the
astonishingly good to the pretty bad but one of
the most noticeable aspects has been the pace of
change.

From its lonely place in the culinary desert,
Birmingham is fast getting the choice of eateries a
nation's second city deserves. The numbers of
new places have been such that at times, some
have wondered if the city can sustain this sort
of growth.

I believe Birmingham can support any number of
quality restaurants. I only wish it would stop
supporting so many mediocre ones.

Some sort of shaking down is inevitable but
the survival rate of new restaurants is generally
scary everywhere and if Birmingham loses one
or two along the way, we shouldn't write off
its foodie ambitions.

As a dining community, we are getting more
sophisticated thanks to this ever-burgeoning
choice. We aren't just the land of the balti any
more, much loved though that speciality is.
(Actually, I suspect those bargain sweet centres
may have spoiled us with their indecently low
prices and made Brummies hostile to the cost of
going to a 'proper' restaurant.)

Sir Terence Conran famously wrote off the city a
few years ago as a place where "they think TGI
Fridays is gastronomy". (I think that was once the
case, sadly - although what choice did we   have
at the time?) But we now know a thing
or two about quality, innovation and service and
as our knowledge increases, so our standards rise.

Birmingham is alive at the moment with the buzz of optimism, of new development, of the sense of new opportunities. At the time of writing, more exciting new developments are heading this way - Heathcotes, Chez Gerard and Livebait all promise much.
Even Conran is coming. The city's culinary map is being rewritten month by month,
year by year.

Many of these new ventures are chains, albeit some rather classy ones. Birmingham is dominated by the corporate big guys and we could really do with more little chef-patron places - Didier Philipot's La Toque d'Or in Hockley is a fine example - but could anyone afford to set up shop in the city now without the massive wads of big commerce behind them?

This area is changing and I believe the national restaurant guides give it a pretty poor service. I hope this effort helps put
that to rights. It's not meant to be a comprehensive list of every restaurant and pub around but every place which gains entry has something of interest to offer.
The particularly good places get a star; the outstandingly good get two stars.

You won't agree with all my assessments, I'm sure, but I hope that it will at least help the area's many visitors through the maze and guide the people who live here to some new favourites.

Alison Davison
August 2001

ACKNOWLEDGEMENTS

I owe a debt of gratitude to Laurence McCoy,
Mandy McGeever, Paul Fulford, Sally Orton, Jayne
Howarth and Keith Dickinson. But my biggest
thank-you must go to Jeremy Bowen,
of Stratford-upon-Avon cheesemongers Paxton
and Whitfield, for his tidal wave of enthusiasm,
help and encouragement.

For
Laurie
and
Amelia.

Text © Alison Davison
All rights reserved

This publication may not be reproduced in whole or
in part, translated, stored in a retrieval system or
transmitted or distributed in any form or by means
(electronic, mechanical, photocopy, recording, printed
or otherwise) without the prior written consent of the
publisher or under a valid licence for limited copying
issued by the Copyright Licensing Agency Ltd.

First published in 2001 by
Astoria Publishing Ltd, 147 High Street,
Henley in Arden, Warwickshire, B95 5BA
Telephone - 01564 196363
Email - info@astoriapublishing.co.uk
www.astoriapublishing.co.uk

ISBN 1-903802-01-6
Typeset by Blue Moon, Evesham, Worcestershire
Printed by Vale Press Ltd, Willersey, Worcs. WR12 7RR

CONTENTS

UNDERSTANDING MENUSPEAK

Is the menu full of funny words you don't understand? Don't worry – hardly anybody but classically-trained chefs knows what the hell they mean either and often they're there just to sound good. But if your curiosity and nagging sense of inferiority are keeping you awake at nights, here are the textbook definitions.

Aïoli. A garlic mayonnaise from Provence.

Arigula. Rocket.

Ballotine. Meat, game bird, poultry, possibly fish, in aspic. The flesh is usually boned, rolled and wrapped in muslin before being poached or braised.

Barigoule. À la barigoule is a way of stuffing and braising globe artichokes, traditionally with mushrooms, fatty bacon and ham.

Bavarois. Cold, gelatine-set dessert made from egg custard mixed with whipped cream and flavourings.

Beignets. Fritters made with batter, choux pastry or dough.

Beurre blanc. A sauce made with reduced vinegar, shallots and butter.

Blanquette. Ragout (see below) of white meat (poultry, lamb or often veal) cooked in aromatic, flavoured white stock or water. Sometimes has a roux of egg yolk and cream.

Blini. Small savoury pancake.

Boudin blanc. White-meat sausage. Regions of France have their own variations.

Boulangere. Fish or lamb cooked à la boulangere traditionally means oven-baked with potatoes and chopped onions.

Brandade. Salt cod, olive oil and milk, often in a purée and sometimes with garlic.

Cassoulet. A stew of haricot beans cooked with meat. The three traditional types are based on either pork, mutton and/or partridge and a mix of mutton with any or all of the following -

duck, goose, lard or Toulouse sausage. But vegetarian bean stews are now popping up named cassoulets.

Ceps. Or cèpes or porcini or penny buns. A delicious mushroom variety.

Ceviche. Raw fish marinated in lemon juice and dished up with raw onion rings, sweetcorn and tomatoes.

Charmoula. A thick sweet and sour sauce used in Arab cooking, using a spicy ragout of onions, honey, vinegar and raisins.

Chiffonade. Strips of sorrel, chicory or lettuce, possibly softened in butter with cream or stock added. Used to garnish soup.

Clafoutis. Dessert of fruit, often cherries, baked in a sweet batter.

Colcannon. Irish dish of mashed potato with cabbage and chives.

Coppa. Cured Italian or Corsican pork marinated in red wine and garlic.

Coulis. A liquid purée.

Croustade. Pastry case (can also be made of bread or potato).

Daube. Meat braised in a herby, red wine stock.

Duxelles. A stuffing or garnish made of chopped mushrooms, shallots and onion sautéed in butter.

Escabèche. Cold, spicy marinade for preserving cooked food, particularly small fish.

Escalope. Thin slice of white meat.

Farçi. Basically it means stuffed and usually refers to cabbage leaves filled with forcemeat, traditionally cooked in stock.

Feuilleté. Pastry with a savoury filling or garnish.

Fritto misto. Assortment of savoury fritters.

Galantine. Dish of pressed, lean pieces of meat mixed with forcemeat, cooked in aspic stock and served cold.

Galette. A round flat cake, a crepe or a biscuit.

Granita. Italian sorbet, very granular and often made with coffee.

Gribiche. Mayonnaise-like cold sauce.

Jambonette. Traditionally, cooked charcuterie made from pork shoulder and bacon, moulded into a pear shape.

Jus. Pan juices diluted (often with stock) and boiled to get all the pan flavours in.

Nage. A sauce, usually with scallops, langoustes, small lobsters or crayfish, made from the seasoned stock, or court bouillon, in which the food is cooked, sometimes with cream added. ('À la nage' means 'swimming')

Navarin. Ragout (see below) usually of mutton or lamb and often with spring vegetables.

Pain d'épice. Gingerbread in the French style, with honey and spices.

Palmier. Small, sugared, palm-shaped pastry.

Pan-bagnat. Bread spread with olive oil and made into a sandwich with savoury fillings such as anchovy, olives and onion.

Parfait. Iced dessert to which cream has been added for smoothness and so it can slice more easily.

Paupiette. A little roll of meat spread with forcemeat, secured with a cocktail stick and braised or fried.

Pavé. A slab or block and refers to anything from blocks of cake or gingerbread to thick pieces of prime beef.

Pistou. A Provençal version of pesto made by grinding basil with garlic and olive oil.

Pithiviers. Round puff pastry pastie traditionally filled with almond cream.

Pot au feu. Classic French one-pot stew of meat, veg and broth.

Quenelles. Dumplings, usually of spiced meat or fish (eels especially).

Ragout. A stew of same-sized pieces of meat, fish, poultry, game or vegetables cooked in a thickened, often herby liquid without being browned first.

Rouille. Sauce from Provence for fish and fish soup made from chillies, garlic and breadcrumbs (or potato) with olive oil and stock.

Rillettes. A potted, smooth paste made from rabbit, pork, goose or poultry cooked in lard.

Sabayon. Frothy sauce, often made with champagne, typically for shellfish or fish. Sabayon also means zabaglione, the Italian dessert.

Sarladaise. Potatoes à la sarladaise are sliced thinly, sautéed in goose fat and sprinkled with parsley and garlic.

Savarin. Big rum-flavoured, ring-shaped gateau of baba dough (without raisins) filled with cream.

Turron. A sort of Spanish nougat of ground almonds, egg whites and sugar. It may contain pistachios, dried fruit, perhaps walnuts or almonds.

Vacherin. Can mean either a seasonal cheese (from France or Switzerland) or a ring dessert made from meringue or almond paste filled with ice cream.

Velouté. Can be a sauce or soup. As a sauce, it's one of the classics and based on chicken or white veal stock or sometimes a fish fumet (reduced stock) thickened with a roux (a mix of flour and fat). A velouté soup is thickened with egg yolks, cream and butter.

These are a few of my favourite places or those I've been most impressed by (in no particular order of preference).

BIRMINGHAM'S TOP 10 RESTAURANTS

La Toque d'Or

Denial

Bank

Bay Tree

Le Petit Blanc

Marriott Hotel (both Langtry's and the Sir Edward Elgar)

Quod

Wing Wah

Metro Bar and Grill

TOP 10 OUTSIDE BIRMINGHAM

Simpsons, Kenilworth

Bilash, Wolverhampton

Corse Lawn Hotel, near Tewkesbury

Marsh Goose, Moreton-in-Marsh

Hibiscus, Ludlow

Merchant House, Ludlow

Mr Underhill's, Ludlow

Mallory Court, near Leamington

Venture In, Ombersley

Desports, Stratford-upon-Avon

TOP 10 PUBS FOR FOOD

Waterdine, Llanfair Waterdine

Crabmill, Preston Bagot, near Henley-in-Arden

Bell and Cross, Clent

The Boot, Lapworth

Churchill Arms, Paxford

Crown and Sandys, Ombersley

Eight Bells, Chipping Campden

King's Head, Aston Cantlow

Three Crowns Inn, Ullingswick

Riverside Inn, Aymestrey

10 TO DRESS UP FOR

Put on your best frocks (you too girls) and check your plastic can take the strain.

Buckland Manor, Buckland, Glos

Marriott Hotel, Sir Edward Elgar, Birmingham

New Hall Hotel, Sutton Coldfield

Mallory Court, near Leamington Spa

Lords of the Manor, Glos

No 1 Pimlicos, Stratford-upon-Avon

Castle House Hotel, Hereford

La Rive, Hereford

Brockencote Hall, Chaddesley Corbett

Chavignol at the Old Mill, Shipston-on-Stour, Warks

VEGETARIAN DELIGHTS

They may be modest but these vegetarian restaurants offer tasty, filling food at bargain prices.

The Warehouse Café, Birmingham

Café at All Saints, Hereford

Jyoti, Birmingham

Samosa, Birmingham

Rogans, Birmingham

ABBERLEY

The Elms

Stockton Road, Abberley, Worcs, WR6 6AT.
01299 896666. Fax 01299 896804.
Website: www.theelmshotel.co.uk

Modern English

Every day
12-2, 7-9.

CC (slips left open),
Wheelchair access.
Local produce.
2 V.

L £10 - 2 courses,
£15 - 3 courses.

D £34.95 -
3 courses.

Abberley is a particularly lovely part of Worcestershire and the Elms, the sort of grand old building which regularly appears in BBC costume dramas, is a particularly lovely destination.

Inevitably, such a venue has found a reliable income in the wedding biz but private diners should still seek it out when their souls need the solace of a soothing view across green, undulating hills and their spirits require a quick tonic (with gin, ice and lemon please) in the comfy sofas of the welcoming bar before a slap-up meal.

The owners also have the prestigious Buckland Manor in the Cotswolds so you imagine the sort of oak-panelled, soft-carpeted world you're in - although I haven't found the Elms to match up to Buckland's ethereal standards on my visits.

But there's still a pampering time to be had in the chintzy, spacious dining room with its botanical prints and solidly upholstered chairs. Starters may feature a grand soup of seared Cornish scallops, watercress and potato or duck foie gras terrine with toasted brioche and spiced pear chutney. The main courses offer some twists on the classics, like a pot au feu with lamb shank rather than beef or pan-fried petit sirloin of Scotch beef with polenta and a red wine and shallot sauce.

ALDERMINSTER

Ettington Park Hotel ★

Alderminster, near Stratford-upon-Avon,
Warks, CV37 8BU.
01789 450123. Fax 01789 450472.
Email: ettington@arcadianhotels.co.uk
Website: www.arcadianhotels.co.uk

Modern British
Every day
7-9.30.
Sun
12-2

CC. (slips closed)
Wheelchair access
(+WC).
2 V.

£32.50 - 3 courses
(+ supplements).
+a/c

An immense gothic pile just outside Stratford with the ruins of a 12th century church in its elegant grounds ... hmm, would that appeal to American tourists perhaps? Especially as this particular listed beauty has a history going back 800 years and also is rather blessed with tales of ghostly goings-on - a lady in grey, echoes of crying children, mysteriously clicking billiard balls. You know the sort of thing.

But it's not just a temporary home for transatlantic visitors; it has more than its fair share of celeb guests too (the Spice Girls all stayed here in their Geri heyday), being rather convenient for the NEC.

The large grounds, patrolled by peacocks, are delightful; there are tables on the terrace so you can enjoy a sunlit gin and tonic on a lovely evening and take in the scenery. Or perhaps a leisurely sunny lunch.

Service is careful and polite and the food on offer in the formal, rather hushed dining room is cooking in the grand hotel style - generally textbook, gracious stuff, elaborately presented and designed as much to fulfil expectations as to please.

It's all perfectly fine with a very pleasant sense of being well looked after. Prices, for wine too, match the grandeur of the building.

> "I presume the lady's driving the way you're knocking it back" – Charming waiter to Ms Davison's companion

ALVECHURCH

The Mill ★

Radford Road, Alvechurch, Worcs B48 7LD.
0121 447 7005. Fax 0121 447 8001.

Fans of the Lebanese wine Chateau Musar would have a whale of a time here with a wine list that includes a whole subsection devoted to vintages from 1964.

It may seem an unusual choice for this cosy, almost domestic restaurant tucked away in a rather grand brick building just away from the main road, where the food sticks to tried and tested favourites.

Classical/modern English and French

Tues-Thurs 7-8.30, Fri 7-9,

Sat 7-9.30.

CC (no Diners; slips left open). Free range/organic produce. 1 V.

Tues-Fri £17.50 - 2 courses, £19.50- 3 courses.

Sat £26.50 - 3 courses.

Solid, reliable stuff is what goes down well here and the McKinnon family who own and run the place, know better than to waste valuable menu space with more avant garde dishes that won't sell.

Still, it's hardly a second class option to stick to sturdy favourites combined with familiar contemporary flavours. Chicken breast may get spinach, white wine and asparagus, there is rosemary with lamb shank and tomato, chilli and black olives with sea bass. A loyal fan base ensures the homely touch; this is a friendly place with no airs and graces.

ALVESTON

No1 Pimlicos ★

Pimlico Lane, Alveston, near Stratford-upon-Avon, Warks, CV37 7RF.
01789 295510. Fax 01789 292961.

Modern European.

Every day 12.30-3, 6-10.30.

CC (slips left open). Wheelchair access (+WC). A/C.

The old Baraset Barn was a bit of a fave not just with the locals but with Birmingham folk who wanted a bit of a run out to make an evening feel special. That closed due to the head honcho's retirement and it has since undergone an amazing transformation from 80s barn-style conversion to this cutting edge modern restaurant that would grace any well-heeled, central London street.

It's still expensive but obviously the market here willingly supports it. And look what you get for it - apart from the tables in the revamped original section (which is now partly a gorgeous new bar), there's an extension, the Orangery, with tan leather chairs, crisply-clothed tables and smart roof blinds keeping the sun off some expensive hairdos. It really is the biz.

Thank goodness the food's good too. The dishes here are real quality - not hugely complicated but with decent ingredients and an able enough grasp of the basics to make a success of beautifully-cooked fish, meat and pasta. The portions will not overwhelm you and it's all rather effortless and clever.

Service was willing; an excellent venue with excellent food.

Local produce.
1V.
Starters
£3.25-£6.25.
Mains
£10.95-£16.95.
Desserts
£4.25-£5.25.
Mon-Fri L,
£9.95 - 3 courses.
Sun L
£21.95 - 3 courses.
£19.95 - 2 courses.

ARMSCOTE

Fox and Goose ★

Armscote, Stratford-upon-Avon.
Warks, CV37 8DD. 01608 682293.
Website: www.foxandgoose.co.uk

Youthful, trendy things go on inside this redbrick village pub not far from Bardsville.

Stripped wooden flooring, rustic old pine tables and a gentle cream exterior are a sure sign of its foodie intentions. The tempting selection chalked up on the blackboard travels the world in style, from smoked goose to gravadlax with blinis to lamb koftas.

The atmosphere is buzzy - it's popular and understandably so, as hearty, quality food is

Modern British
Every day
12-2.30, 7-9.30.
CC (no Diners; slips left open).
Wheelchair access (+WC).
Local produce.
3 V.
Starters
£3.50-£5.50.
Mains
£8.75-£12.50.
Desserts
£3-£4.50.

reliably on the cards. Tuck into a starter of good seafood terrine or go for broke with calves' liver on red wine jus and bubble and squeak or pig out on homemade pasta wrapped round sweet roast peppers and goat's cheese and dressed with an excellent, zingy pesto. The classics get a twist in the pud section too - an apricot bread and butter pudding made with croissants and brioche and a creme anglaise showing a happy anglo-French marriage. Prices are sensible.

There are also rooms available and the decor in the rest of the building can go a little, well, safari style. The ladies loos, for instance, were decked out in zebra patterns and purple. Eat your heart out, Laurence Llewelyn Bowen.

ASTON CANTLOW

King's Head ★

Bearley Road, Aston Cantlow,
near Stratford-upon-Avon, Warks, B95 6HY.
01789 488242. Fax 01789 488137.
Email: thekingshead@amserve.net

Modern British

Mon-Sat
12-2.30, 7-10.

Sun
12.30-3, 7-9.

CC (no Diners; slips
left open).
Wheelchair access
(+WC).
2 V.

Starters
£3.25-£6.95.

Mains
£8.95-£14.95.

Desserts
£4.50.

Set menus for
groups.

This popular country pub (one of local maestro Paul Salisbury's) regularly packs them in, especially at weekends, when booking is essential.

The village of Aston Cantlow is very pretty and the pub is well-placed within it, right next to the very scenic church. It's an old (15th century) black and white inn but offbeat lettering on the exterior lets you know that this is no freezer-to-microwave joint.

The interior is as beautifully done out as Salisbury's other places, with a carefully-designed modern rustic look to go with the flagstoned floors and original beams.

Probably the only regular item on the menu is the famous duck supper' which has allegedly been on offer for 20 years (not the same duck, you understand). It's also one of their few traditionalist items, being more like a Sunday roast and served with "smashed roots" and gravy.

The rest of the food is marked by a youthful
exuberance; this is playtime with all the global
flavours they can get their hands on. Orange and
cardamom beurre blanc is the dressing for a whole
grilled plaice, while seared squid comes with chilli
guacamole and even dull old smoked salmon has
olive oil and parmesan. Not everything works 100
per cent (you may suspect that a kitchen working
as flat out as this is bound to slip occasionally)
but it succeeds often enough to keep its army
of punters more than happy. There's a pretty
garden too.

AYMESTREY

Riverside Inn ★

Aymestrey, Herefordshire. HR6 9ST.
01568 708440. Fax 01568 709058.
Email: riverside@aymestrey.fsnet.co.uk
Website: www.theriversideinn.net

The river in question is the Lugg, a sleepy little
waterway which at this point (Aymestrey is a quiet
village between Leominster and Ludlow) provides
a very pretty boundary for the pub's garden.

There are many good reasons for a trip out here:
The countryside is delightful, there's sightseeing
(the National Trust's Berrington Court, gardens to
visit and various historic sights including Croft Castle
and Mortimer's Trail) and the food and drink
are excellent.

The ancient black and white pub, a long, low affair
with parts dating back to the 16th century, has its
own brewery which provides some top-notch ales
(Jack Snipe especially recommended.) The gardens
are also put to use supplying vegetables and herbs
for the kitchen.

The window-walled dining room is non-smoking
and the atmosphere in the bar is great - pubby as
opposed to restauranty and very friendly.

The food may cover a wide range from baguettes
to simple but quality roast dinners to ravioles of

Eclectic with French
influences

Mon-Sat
12-2.30, 7-10.

Sun
12-2.30, 7-9.30.

Local/free range
produce.
CC (no Amex, Diners)
4 V.

Starters
£3.25-£5.95.

Mains
£8.95-£15.95

Desserts
£3.95.

Set menu
£18.95 - 3 courses.

duck. It's ambitious, with local sourcing a particular point of pride (naturally-reared meat sources get a mention). I think we can assume that 'steak, kidney and red kite pie' has none of the last ingredient within it. Other choices may include Herefordshire duckling breast with savoy cabbage, bacon and bramble sauce or rack of Marches lamb with saffron potato and rosemary sauce. Everything is reasonably-priced.

It's a popular haunt for the top Ludlow chefs in their civvies too.

BEARWOOD

Azzari Too . . .

204 Lightwoods Road, Bearwood, Warley, B67 5AZ. 0121 429 6621. Website: www.azzaritoo.co.uk

Global fusion
Tues-Fri
12-2.30, 6-10.30.

Sat
7-10.30.

CC (slips left open).
Wheelchair access.
3 V.

Starters
£2.95-£5.45.

Mains
£7.95-£14.95.

Desserts
£3.25.

Set menu available.

Good neighbourhood eateries don't just make life worthwhile, they make it so much simpler. Can't be bothered to cook? Just pop down the road, no need to dress up, and let someone else slave over a hot stove. The welcome will be warm, the food will fill the gap nicely without causing tidal waves in your bank balance and you'll head home relaxed and happier than when you walked in.

Such a place is Azzari Too (an odd moniker but so called after the daughter of chef-owner Barry Hall).

You couldn't get much more urban than this, nestling on a corner of downtown Bearwood (the site used to be a Michelle's restaurant), just a few steps away from the busy high street (and the Bear pub) and rows of houses stretching away in every other direction.

The canopied, cream exterior, neatly bordered by green hedging, is matched by a calm cream interior, a user-friendly arty place with natural colours, pretty chairs and interesting pictures. A subtly pleasant backdrop for surprisingly global food.

Gnocchi, pasta, roast rib of beef with horseradish, coconut curry, halloumi, Malaysian laksa chicken - all these and more can make an appearance and jolly robust most of it is too. Friendly stuff and proud of it.

BELBROUGHTON

Freshmans

22-26 Church Hill, Belbroughton, Stourbridge, DY9 0D7. 01562 730467. Fax 01562 731478. Email: :info@freshmans-restaurant.co.uk" Website: www.freshmans-restaurant.co.uk

Traditional British

Tues-Sat
7-9.30.

Sun
12-2.

CC (no Amex, Diners, slips closed). Request V when booking.

Starters
£3.50-£6.25.

Mains
£7.95-£15.95.

Desserts
£3.95-£4.95.

Set menus available for groups.

A perfect English village scene awaits the visitor to Freshmans. Its long, quaint building nestles in beautifully next to some equally-picturesque neighbours by the church.

The look inside is traditional too, with beams and prints adding to the olde feel. It's a friendly place and the food also aims to please. Don't expect to lose any weight - smoked chicken is deep-fried in batter for a starter with a spiced olive oil dressing; sardines are coated in flour and grilled; goat's cheese is baked in filo and laid on bacon.

The trend continues with main courses - sugar-coated roast duck breast, brandy-flamed fried pork medallions. Filling and comforting, it may not be the perfect place for a marathon runner's pre-race lunch.

"I am a great eater of beef, and I believe that does harm to my wit" - Shakespeare (Twelfth Night)

BERKSWELL

Nailcote Hall ★

The Oak Room restaurant, Nailcote Lane, Berkswell, Warks, CV7 7DE.
02476 466174. Fax 02476 470720.
Email: info@nailcotehall.co.uk

Traditional English
Every day
12-2, 7-9.30.

CC (slips left open).
Wheelchair access
(+WC).
1 V.

Starters
average £8.95.

Mains
average £24.50.

Desserts
average £5.95.

Set L
£ 21.50 - 3 courses.

D (Mon-Fri)
£29.50 - 3 courses.

Sat
£32.50 - 3 courses.

Sun L
£22.50 - 3 courses.

Nailcote Hall is a stately and impressive black and white place in 15 acres of grounds and its Oak Room restaurant is just one of the attractions on offer - the place is also a hotel/cabaret venue/golf and country club.

Soft lights, beams, polished mahogany tables and silverware all speak romance and opulence - in discreetly hushed tones, of course.

Not a cheap place then - the set menu is £32.50 for three courses or serious boat-pushers can go à la carte. But the food is impressive and as opulent and well-presented as the surroundings.

Delicacy is done well - as in a baby leek and new potato terrine livened up with a vinaigrette dressing, salad and sun-dried tomatoes - and big flavours get a nice balancing act of fruity or sharp contrasts. Amazingly-fresh fish score particularly high marks.

The kitchen's presentational skills really go to town with the desserts, some of which could qualify as modern art.

BIRMINGHAM

Al-Frash

186 Ladypool Road, Sparkbrook, B12 8JS.
0121 753 3120.

Pakistani
Sun-Thurs
5-12.
Fri/Sat
5-1am.

I wouldn't attempt a comprehensive list of Birmingham balti houses. I'm just going to mention a handful which are particular favourites and hope I don't upset too many people.

Al-Frash, in the heart of Birmingham's balti belt, is a

goodie - brighter-looking than most and very welcoming and professional. Having won several 'top balti' awards, it's understandably always busy.

It's bring your own of course, which makes it even more of a bargain, so you can have a decent tipple while slavering over the possibilities - which, typically, include masses of choice for vegetarians.

Pakoras, perhaps of aubergine or potato, are crisp on the outside and meltingly, spicily soft within. Excellent house specialities feature such fragrant wonders as king prawns in garlic and chilli scattered with fresh coriander and strewn with almonds and pistachios.

Spicing is careful and the food tastes reassuringly fresh. The kulfi is recommended too.

CC.
Wheelchair access.
24 V.

Starters
from 90p.

Mains
from £4.30.

Desserts
from £1.30.

Set menu for
groups

All Bar One

The Water's Edge, Brindleyplace and Newhall Street, city centre. 0121 644 5861 and 0121 212 9991 respectively.

Times shown are for Brindleyplace.

International

Mon-Wed
12-10.

Thurs-Sat
12-12.

Sun
12-9.

All Bar One is a chain but one which manages decently enough to get a listing here.

The trendily-basic bars have lots of bare wood (floors, tables, even old church seats), young staff and a blackboard of food which is something of a lower priority to the buzz of people (often professionals in the case of Newhall Street, a younger crowd at Brindleyplace) enjoying a drink in the laidback, no-fuss surroundings.

CC (no Diners; slips left open).
Wheelchair access (+WC).
A/C.
3 V.

Starters
£3.25-£5.25.

Mains
£5.25-£9.95.

Desserts
£3.50.

Substantial sandwiches - whether panini (with fillings of perhaps brie or smoked cheese and mushroom) or burgers (on ciabatta) - come with fries and salad to make a lunchtime bite big enough to see off the noisiest of rumbling stomachs.

'Plates' on the menu here mean a cooked meal. They sound fine but there can be a discrepancy between what's written and what appears on the plate. Roasted Med veg with buttered mash and red pesto, for instance, came without the pesto.

Seared teriyaki salmon with udon noodles, lemon grass, chilli and ginger actually came with peppers - and none of the more oriental flavourings in sight (except some soy sauce).

Reasonably-priced filling food, then, to help soak up some of the alcohol. Worth a visit for the feelgood ambience.

B3 bar and restaurant

12-22 Edmund House, Newhall Street, city centre, B3 3LX.
0121 236 7879. Fax 0121 236 7950.

Eclectic

Mon-Wed
12-10.

Thurs/Fri
12-2am.

Sat
6-2am.

CC (no Solo; slips left open).
Wheelchair access (+WC).
A/C.
4 V.

Starters
£3.95-£5.50.

Mains
£6.95-£11.95.

Desserts
£3.80

Next door to its sibling nightclub (B2), B3 looks the part in its impressive if rather sombre commercial sector surroundings.

The largely glass frontage, lots of mirrors and neatly draped tables in subdued colours all say modern in a nicely discreet way.

The menu covers all the expected bases - risotto, Caesar salad, focaccia, Thai-style noodles et al. Service is friendly enough but the food standards can be variable - pasta in a tomato and creme fraiche sauce was tasty and surprisingly spicy but a lacklustre 'salad of two pears' failed to win any fans. Swordfish was nicely cooked and served with a mountain of chips (choose either fat or thin varieties).

The gluttonous feel continues into dessert with deep-fried ice cream available. It's OK - not quite the indulgent hit you may expect - but definitely one for the skinnies.

"Maybe the landlord will be forgiving. After all, Ms Davison is female and clearly it was a bad time of the month for her" - Letter to The Birmingham Post

Bank ★

4 Brindleyplace, Birmingham. B1 2JB.
0121 633 4466. Fax 0121 633 4465.
Email: info@bankbirmingham.co.uk

Liberated French

Mon-Thurs
7.30-10.30am,
12-3, 5.30-11.

Fri
7.30am-10.30am,
12-3, 5.30-11.30.

Sat
11-3, 5.30-11.30.

Sun
11-5.

CC (slips left open).
Wheelchair access
(+WC).
A/C
5 V.

Starters
£4.50-£10.50.

Mains
£10-£32.

Desserts
£4.25-£6.

Set menu
(£9.95 – 2 courses,
£12.50 – 3 courses)
at certain times.

The arrival of Bank in Birmingham saw the city's first experience of a food factory and a stylish one at that. A big, ultra-modern eaterie, the service from the Mao-suited, professional staff is slick, the food spot-on and the experience buzzy - sometimes too much so. All those hard surfaces - the terrifying sheets of glass hanging vertically from the ceiling, the bold-coloured walls, the moulded concrete - bounce the noise around to high levels at times, particularly on hectic weekend nights.

So, not the venue for a romantic twosome perhaps (unless you get there early before the hordes arrive) but an impressively good place to eat all the same. The food covers an excellent range of cuisines and price levels, from the dish which now pops up everywhere - seared, oriental-flavoured tuna - to fish and chips (excellent) and from confit duck leg with sauteed potatoes and sauce vierge to roast quail with wild mushroom and herb risotto. You can rest easy that the wealth of choice is manageable in a kitchen staffed by so many (it's on full view behind the bar).

You don't have to eat at Bank - many enjoy a drink at the long central bar before moving on to sample the rest of this hugely popular area. It's also open for breakfast and coffees and does a great Sunday brunch where you can sit with the papers (the chairs are nicely comfy) and spot local celebs.

Executive chef Idris Caldora made his name earlier in his career with an award-winning stint at what was then the Swallow Hotel. Bank food is simpler of course but that sense of quality and sharp culinary imagination is evident throughout.

Bay Tree ★

27 Chad Square, Hawthorne Road,
Edgbaston, Birmingham. B15 3TQ.
0121 455 6697. Fax 0121 454 4335.
Website: www.the-bay-tree-restaurant.co.uk

Modern British.
Mon-Fri
12-2.30, 7-10.30.

Sat
7-10.30.

Sun 12-2.30.

CC
(slips left open).
Wheelchair
access (+WC).
A/C.
Organic/free
range.
6 V.

L - £5 per course.

Table d'hote
dinner -
£14.95 - 2 courses,
£17.50 - 3 courses.

Alc
£21.95 - 2 courses.
£24.95 - 3 courses.

The arrival of chef Andy Waters from Michelin-
starred Simpsons in Kenilworth has really put this
smart suburban eaterie on the map.

It's been refurbished and with its new-look little
bar and elegant dining area, the look of the place
is up to the level of the food. It can be quiet but
hopefully it is finally getting the support it
deserves. The catchment area is pretty damned
good after all. This is fine dining and upmarket
food - but the prices are nowhere near as scary as
you'd expect with £5 a course at lunch and two
courses for £12.95 or three at £15.50 at dinner.
Cheap at the price for pan-fried John Dory with a
'provence' of vegetables and deep-fried scallops
or a duo of duck and pork with braised red
cabbage in a green peppercorn sauce.

The choices for vegetarians are excellent. They might
include grilled asparagus tart with parmesan, rocket
and truffle oil, pastilla of roasted winter vegetables
on braised lentils with thyme butter nage or ravioli
of blue cheese with a salad of celery, apples and
witloof topped with a walnut vinaigrette - it makes
you hungry just thinking about it.

If you know Simpsons food, you'll be in familiar
territory here - loads of expertly-handled flavours,
real vibrancy of taste - slightly more robust,
possibly. Satisfying food to remember.

The Bucklemaker

30 Mary Ann Street, Hockley, B3 1RL.
0121 200 2515. Fax 0121 236 9887.
Website: www.thebucklemaker.co.uk

Modern British
Mon-Fri
12-2.30, 5.30-10.30.

Sat
7-10.30.

C (slips left open).

Many Bucklemaker clients are professionals from
the nearby city centre who flee here for a quick
respite from the cut and thrust. It certainly

feels like a bolthole, with its modest frontage hiding a discreet staircase which takes you down to what is almost the 70s stereotype of a wine bar - dark wooden bar, bare brick walls and wrought iron panels.

There's a lot of choice on offer and some nice dishes but carelessness can creep in. A tartlet of goat's cheese and aubergine was pleasant but a main course of half a butternut squash topped with vegetables was unexciting and expensive (£9.25). A perfectly acceptable main course of monkfish was let down by side dishes (all extras) of green beans scattered with burnt, acrid garlic and stringy spinach.

A/C.
4 V.

Starters
£3.50-£7.50.

Mains
£8.50-£22.50.

Desserts
£4.95.

Set L
£12.50 - 2 courses.

Buonissimo

1 Albany Road, Harborne, B17 9JX.
0121 426 2444. Fax 0121 428 2465.

Bustling little Buonissimo has built up a regular local trade with its easy-living food served up in smart yet relaxed, youthful surroundings.

With its white, glass shelves, spotlights and plain mirrors, it offers a modernist, feelgood café space with food that's informal and out to satisfy rather than impress. It also gets away from that osso-bucco stereotype of Italian restaurant food with tempting dishes such as risottos with saffroned onions, aubergine and rocket or lemon and basil-marinated chicken breast with a crisp salad.

Mornings see coffee and pastries on the menu while mealtimes have good-value, set-price lunches and sensible à la carte. The upstairs eating area (the Mediterranean Room) is available for overspill during busy times.

Dishes such as slow-braised lamb shank with a red wine and rosemary jus and big pasta specialities are hefty but strong on flavour. Laudably, they have some dishes available in children's portions at half price so you can avoid the nuggets and chips mentality.

Puds are soothing and the wine list is short, fairly cheap and predictable.

Modern Italian

Tues-Sat
10.30-2.15, 6-10.15.

Mon 6-10.15.

CC (slips left open).
Organic/free range.
3 V.

Starters under £5

Mains under £10.

Desserts
£2.95-£3.50.

Set L menus and
for groups.

Burlington Hotel ★

Berlioz, Burlington Arcade, 126 New Street, B2 4JQ. 0121 633 1737. Fax: 0121 643 3075. Email: berlioz@burlingtonhotel.com

Eclectic
Mon-Sat
12-2.30, 6.30-10.

Sun (carvery)
1-2, 6.30-9.30.

CC
(slips left open).
Wheelchair access
(+WC).
A/C.
3 V.

Starters
£5.75-£9.

Mains
£14.25-£19.95.

Desserts
£4.95-£5.50.

Set menu
£15.95 – 2 courses,
£19.95 – 3 courses.

Quietly swish surroundings are the rule here in this spot which was once so central but can now feel slightly out of the way with all the to-do at Brindleyplace and the Mailbox. At least it must cut down their formal competition in the near vicinity.

The comfortable, upholstered chairs, formally-draped tables and dramatically-curtained tall windows all speak well-to-do hotel.

A couple of inspection meals have been marred by service blips - a great shame as the welcome is fine and the food very good.

The menu is international with no fear of surprisingly exotic combinations but the spicing and mixing of flavours is deft and well-balanced. Eastern tastes such as ginger and soy are handled well, especially in partnership with steamed salmon and mussels on good, crunchy pak choi (the vegetables are cooked carefully), where all is lightness and delicacy. Puddings are as indulgent as any sugar-craver could wish.

Café Ikon ★

The Ikon Gallery, 1 Oozells Square, Brindleyplace, B1 2HS. 0121 248 3226.

Contemporary
Spanish

Tues-Sat
11-11.

Sun
12-3.

CC
(no Amex, Diners;
slips closed).
Wheelchair access
(+WC).
A/C.
Third of menu V.

Tapas/raciones
£1-£7.50.

Paellas
£9-£14.

I've yet to meet anyone who doesn't like Café Ikon. It's impossible not to, I've decided; it just feels good.

A bijou place in the cutting edge Ikon Gallery, its style is impeccable - white, modern, simple lines but with lots of clever touches to make the place feel beautifully comfortable and vibrant. If you're looking for great decor ideas, don't bother with regular interior designers - go along here to get a few tips.

The food - Spanish with the emphasis most definitely on tapas - hits the same happy blend of trendy and fun and is simply made for sharing. Forget the burger joint; if the children are hungry bring them to the Ikon. Tapas are the original children's portions and there's bound to be something they'll eat among the range of tortillas, patatas bravas and spicily robust vegetable or fish or seafood mixes. Meaty stuff pops up as well.

Chilli-wusses should beware but there's lots of help available for the uninitiated. Just order a selection and tuck in.

If you aren't in the mood for lots of nibbles, go straight for the paellas, of which there are several versions available, including vegetarian. These are for a minimum of two.

The quality is excellent, the service youthful and friendly. The café also has a great outlook on a sculpture-dotted bit of Brindleyplace space. Art and food - what could be better?

Café Lazeez

116 Wharfside Street, the Mailbox, B1 1RF.
0121 643 7979. Fax: 0121 643 4546.
Email: lazbirmingham@cs.com
Website: www.cafelazeez.com

Remember The Jetsons, that 60s 'futuristic' cartoon series? I reckon the design of Café Lazeez is partially based on that. This is Indian food, contemporary style, with looks and prices to match.

Café Lazeez, so we can gather, is competition for Shimla Pinks rather than the Sparkbrook balti houses. The look is without doubt bang up-to-date modern - in a rather 60s retro sense of course.

But the food is good, clearly fresh, if fearsomely spicy in parts (and of course, you never know which parts until you take a mouthful). 'Traditional' and 'evolved' Indian dishes share both menu space and an emphasis on quality.

A pretty starter of hot vegetable chaat was tasty but caused several sharp intakes of breath, as did the sausage-like lamb seekh gilafi.

Desserts
£3.25-£4.95.

Modern north Indian/Punjabi.

Mon-Sat
11-1am.

Sun
11-11.30pm.

Wheelchair access (+WC).
A/C.
CC (slips closed)
5+ V.

Starters
£3-£11.

Mains
£7-£15.

Desserts
£3-£5.

Set menus:
L
£9.95 - 2 courses.

Cocktail canapés menu from £10.

Set and buffet menus from £14.95.

Main courses from the "evolved" list are pricier than the traditional and have sparky ideas such as almond-spiked tilapia or Malabar pepper prawns coated in salsa. An 'aubergine delight' was exactly that, a real treat, and cumin-crusted sea bass also proved that modern and traditional could merge very tastefully.

This is the first Café Lazeez outside London and there are clearly high hopes for it, from the interior featuring a long stylish bar, deep red ceiling and trendy seating arrangements, to the beautiful china and stylish cutlery. The wine list is decent too.

Its rather less appealing metropolitan ideas include a discretionary 12.5 per cent service, unisex loos and a charge for the rather good chutneys put on the table with your popadoms.

Casa Paco

7 Fletchers Walk, Paradise Place,
city centre, B3 3HJ .
0121 233 1533.

Spanish
Mon-Thurs
12-2.30, 6.30-10.30.
Fri/Sat
6.30-11.
CC
(slips left open).
Wheelchair access.
A/C.
5 V.
Starters
£2.25-£6.95.
Mains
£6.45-£20.
Desserts
£2.75-£3.75.
Set menus for groups,
£16.50-£25.

If the suggested demolition and redevelopment of Paradise Circus gets the go-ahead, I wonder what on earth will happen to Casa Paco?

So what if it isn't Brindleyplace-style or aiming for Michelin stars - this modest, unassuming bistro serves a purpose and serves it well. Reasonable food in a cosy, homely atmosphere is what we all want from time to time.

From big, busty paellas to unctuous tortillas to tons of steak to gutsy hueva flamenco (baked egg with Serrano ham), this is real grub, filling and big on flavour.

Don't expect gourmet pretensions, wine lists to send Jilly Goolden into orbit or a decor from Homes and Gardens. We're in a strange subterranean spot under a busy traffic island with red gingham tablecloths, waiters who may well address all comments to the male diner rather than his senorina and white walls which are as rough-plastered as some of the customers.

Not that it's yobbish - not at all. It's just latino-style vociferous with more of a continental feel than any pasta chain dreams of attaining.

And the music is pretty splendid too. At the weekend if you're lucky, there may be authentic Spanish guitarists and singers.

Cathay

86 Holloway Head, B1 1NB.
0121 666 7788. Fax 0121 622 2688.

Birmingham's newest oriental restaurant is a stunner - both in strikingly modern looks and in cuisine. Half of the menu in this pale wood, stylish eaterie is zippily fresh, luxurious but quite straightforward fare - predominantly fish and seafood but with some meat and poultry thrown in.

The other half - the 'specialist vegetarian food' - is positively bewildering. Here we have veggie dishes, made from presumably some sort of oriental Quorn, that exactly ape carnivorous classics - there are veggie king prawns, Vietnamese pork, Cathay duck, shark fin soup ... the list is enormous (nine starters, four entrèes, 13 main courses).

How do they do it? They won't say much beyond the menu's claim that the 'meat' is made from fungi and vegetables but it's debatable whether vegetarians may want to eat something which looks and tastes like actual flesh. The degree of attention to detail - a wooden 'bone' in the 'chicken' drumstick even - may seem nauseous to some but it's undeniably curious. The 70s nut cutlet gone mad.

This sort of cooking - known as 'So', as in 'So' chicken, 'So' beef etc - was apparently created by Buddhists to tempt meat-eaters away from their gruesome ways, which perhaps explains it: It was never meant to appeal to vegetarians in the first place.

The genuine non-veg dishes seem guaranteed to please but the vegetarian jury's still out on 'So'. And incidentally, does this mean the Chinese think the TV show So Graham Norton actually features a non-flesh version of the real thing?

Contemporary Chinese/vegetarian

Mon-Thurs
12-2.30, 5.30-11.

Fri/Sat
12-2.30, 5.30-11.30.

Sun
12-2.30.

CC
(slips left open).
Wheelchair access
(+WC).
A/C.
Organic.
14+ V.

Starters
£3.85-£6.95.

Mains
£7.50-£16.00.

Desserts
£3-£3.50.

Set menus
£22.

Chung Ying ★

16-18 Wrottesley Street, Birmingham B5 4RT.
0121 622 5669. Fax: 0121 666 7051
Email: chungying@aol.com
Website: www.chungying.co.uk

Cantonese.
Mon-Sat
12-12,
Sun
12-11pm.
CC
(slips left open).
A/C.
15 V.
Starters
£2-£15.
Mains
£7.50-£16.
Desserts
£2.20-£3.50.
Set menus
£28-£108

The old Brummie favourite may face a lot of eastern competition these days but it remains the Chinese of choice for many when in the heart of the city.

It occupies an imposing corner building in Chinatown and covers two large floors - a huge amount of space, a huge number of diners (and it nearly always seems full) and a menu listing at least 300 dishes.

Where do you start? For the adventurous, there are the steamed duck webs, fish-head soups and various pieces of fried or steamed intestine. Even the more west-friendly dishes can sound rather alarming, such as beef-ball dumplings (and you never know, they just might be).

There's also plenty to play it safe with, including light, delicious king prawns in feather-light pastry or yuk shung with no yuk about it, just shreds of very garlicky crisp chicken with noodles to pack the lettuce leaves with.

Some dishes may seem quite fatty but remain deeply, unctuously flavoursome. Or there can be a happy play of tastes and textures with fried duck with green peppers in black bean sauce.

It's very sociable food of course and this is a very business-like environment (which can get smoky). Service from the army of speedy waiters can be anything from charming to brusque and the bright lights and long, busy tables can make it a less than cosy venue.

"I'm only a beer teetotaller, not a champagne teetotaller" –
George Bernard Shaw (Candida)

Chung Ying Garden

17 Thorp Street, city centre, B5 4AT.
0121 666 6622. Fax 0121 622 5860.
Email/website as above.

Cantonese
Mon-Sat
12-12.

Sun
12-11.

CC
(slips left open).
Wheelchair access
(+WC).
A/C.
20 V.

Starters
£2.20-£15.

Mains
£6-£28.

Desserts
£1.50-£3.50.

Set menus available
£16-£23.

This little sister to the mighty Chung Ying was opened back in 1987 and despite the fact that it's big enough to host several office parties all at the same time (upstairs and downstairs), it likes to think that it's a good place for couples too.

Couples who want to eat well, perhaps, but for a romantic candlelit meal? I don't think so - it's just too big. 'Big tables full of big men' was how one friend described it. At full throttle, this place can seat more than 350 people and the upstairs has karaoke facilities, which doesn't spell romance for me - unless you go all misty-eyed at your loved one crooning Mah Wayyy, of course.

Still, CYG has that lavish style you'd expect in the middle of Chinatown and the lavish choice to go with it. There are more than 90 dim sum dishes as well as oodles of noodles and all the standard favourites besides. You can even choose your meal from a fishtank.

All is reliably well-cooked and efficiently served.

Circo

6-8 Holloway Circus, B1 1BT.
0121 643 1400. Fax 0121 643 6533.
Email: info@circobar.co.uk.

Modern British with
Med touches

Mon-Sat
12-2am.

Sun
noon-12.30am.

CC
(no Diners;
slips left open).
Wheelchair access
(+WC).
2 V.

Starters from £4.

Mains from £5.50.

Desserts from £1.50.

Sun L
£5 - 3 courses.

Trendy bars may be popping up a-hither and a-thither now but Circo can lay claim to being one of the founding fathers, if that doesn't make it feel way too old.

The bar once described by The Sunday Times as being one of the top ten in Britain still looks good, with sawn-off school desks now the order of the day.

But however youthful the looks and however chrome-tastic the space age loos, it's still very matey and down-to-earth, with staff who actually seem happy in their work.

The food's more than decent too, with sandwiches and fries or an oriental stir-fry the reliable lunchtime fare.

Evening food is hearty, stomach-filling and lining stuff, great for clubbers in need of refuelling. Portions are big and well-priced; this is food you'd be chuffed with in a city centre pub.

Wines are few but there's a range of flavoured vodkas behind the bar which probably wipe out most of the world's ills very effectively.

A bargain traditional Sunday lunch of £5 for three courses is definitely worth a try.

City Café ★

City Inn, Brindleyplace, Birmingham B1 2HW.
0121 643 1003.
Email: birmingham.reservations@cityinn.com

Contemporary
Mon-Fri
6.45-9.30am,
12-3,
5.30-11.30.
Sat
7-10am,
11-4,
530-11.30.
Sun
7.30am-4,
5.30-10.30.
CC
(slips left open).
Wheelchair access
(+WC).
2 V.
Starters
£3.50-£7.75.
Mains
£9.25-£15.75.
Desserts
£4.95-£5.25.
Set L
£9.50 - 2 courses.
D
£15.95 - 3 courses.

Fresh, modern, light, good-looking - that's City Café, both in its decor and its food. It has the knowing consultant's eye of TV's troubleshooting chef Pat McDonald about it (his Pershore restaurant, the Epicurean, is listed in a separate entry).

As is the rule with Birmingham's new restaurants, it's a big, big place. Small may be beautiful elsewhere but not, it seems, in the second city.

Lots of glass, strong lines, strong colours against white backdrops, careful design everywhere but very simple and understated, it is the very model of a modern restaurant interior. The one thing it does rather lack is personality but its starkness of spirit may all be part of the master plan for the easy come-easy go race of city diners.

There's an upwardly mobile yet quite simple selection of dishes, with an à la carte and a set menu, which is, off-puttingly, called a 'concept menu'.

It's brasserie stuff, really, but what the flavour combinations may lack in innovation, they make up for both in competent cooking and in the assembly and quality of produce. Goat's cheese and artichoke salad (a starter) becomes special because good ingredients are balanced and dressed properly. Baby tomatoes add sweetness, moist artichoke pieces help give the overall texture succulence and depth while sensible restraint keeps the cheese to two small pieces which don't overbalance the whole and wear out your jaw muscles.

A dish that is pretty much a standby now - seared tuna - is here peppered and served with a light but tasty tomato, basil and coriander salad. The fish is nicely but not frighteningly rare and comes with a salad that contains baby ruby chard and spinach.

Great care is taken over presentation and prices are sensible.

College of Food

Summer Row, city centre, B3 1JB.
0121 604 1010.
Website: www.bcftcs.ac.uk

The young catering students at this busy and highly-regarded college (it also teaches tourism and creative studies) get to try out their stuff in three eateries - the Atrium restaurant, the Brasserie and the Cap and Gown 'pub'.

Careful supervision is on hand at all times as they learn the tricks of serving as well as cooking. It's all rather heart-warming - the shaky hand pouring out your wine, the anxious looks, the gauche manners ... and the staff aren't much better than your nervous new partner.

The food is an absolute bargain - whether it's the grand fare of the Atrium restaurant with its French aspirations and comfy sofas (where I once saw a young trainee stuffing his waistcoat pockets with canapés when he thought no-one was looking) or the no-nonsense bargain lunches of the Brasserie

Term-times only
Atrium
Continental fine dining
Mon-Fri
from 6.30pm.
CC
(no Amex, Diners; slips closed).
A/C.
Wheelchair access (+WC).
1 V.
£12 - 2 courses,
£14 - 3 courses.
Brasserie
International/British
Tues-Fri,
L only (from 12).
As above except:
6 V.
Starters from £2;
mains from £4;
puds from £1.75.

Also set menu.

Cap and Gown

Traditional pub food with oriental touches.

Mon-Fri 12-1.30, from 6.30.

As above except some smoking; 3 V.

Starters from £2; mains from £3.80; puds from £1.75.

(à la carte and table d'hote available), with soups, salads and rustic dishes like chicken chasseur or creamy pastas or pub grub up on the 7th floor.

The decors are less than inspiring but the spirit of enterprise warms the old cockles and what a lovely, lovely thing it is to find yourself in licensed premises where the wine mark-up is a mere £2 or so on the supermarket price. It's almost worth booking yourself a room in town to make the most of it.

The times and hours follow term times and are so restricted that planning ahead is necessary, especially for the Atrium, which gets booked up months ahead.

Continental

Mon-Fri 6.30-10.30am, 12-2.30, 6-11.

Sat 7-11am, 12-2.30, 6-11.

Sun 7-11am, 12-3, 6-11.

CC (slips closed). Wheelchair access (+WC). A/C. 3 V.

Starters £3.25-£7.25.

Mains £7.95-£13.95.

Desserts £3.95-£4.25.

Set D menu £15 - 3 courses.

Sun L carvery £9.95.

Copthorne Hotel

Goldies Brasserie, 1 Paradise Circus, Birmingham B3 3HJ.
0121 200 2727.
Email: sales.birmingham@mill-cop.com

The Copthorne may look a little stranded in its sea of traffic (and facing an uncertain future with plans to demolish Paradise Circus altogether) but it's actually in a very useful spot - straddling Brindleyplace, with its hotspots like the Rep and Symphony Hall, and the rest of the city centre. (Remember that? It's the bit near Brindleyplace and the Mailbox.)

A great spot, then, if unavoidably hotel-ish. But the food is surprisingly good (the competition is inevitably intense around here and all to the good).

The rather sombre setting - all dark wood and hotel carpets - draws on the city's Jewellery Quarter heritage with a theme based on gold and the mining thereof, including some rather unnerving boxed displays of explosives.

The cooking goes for the big bangs too, with a reliance on hearty flavours - French based but with lots of global touches, in a delightfully aromatic tea-smoked duck, for example.

Descriptions tend to the fine dining (millefeuilles with risottos, gateaux of crepes and so on). An excellent vegetarian cassoulet was superb - better than its accompanying tartlet - and fish was generally well cooked too. Big rib-eye steaks also cater for the big of appetite who like to see value for money.

Puds, including some powerful berried concoctions and excellent ice creams, show a similar chasing after flavour at the occasional expense of balance.

Denial ★

120-122 Wharfside Street,
the Mailbox, B1 1RQ.
0121 643 3080.
Email: enquiries@denial.ltd.uk
Website: www.denial.ltd.uk

Eclectic
Mon-Fri
8am-11pm.
Sat
10am-11pm.
Sun
10-10.30.

CC
(no Diners; slips closed).
Wheelchair access (+WC).
A/C.
Free range.
1 V.

L
£10 - 2 courses,
£13 - 3 courses

D
£19.50 - 2 courses,
£23.50 - 3 courses.

Denial was the newest kid on Birmingham's block as we went to press, only opening its trendy doors to the public in summer 2001.

It perches right by a canal cul de sac in a very des res spot just along the way from Fish! and is the only independently-owned restaurant in the Mailbox so far.

The look, as you'd expect, aspires to cutting edge chic. An impressive central bar divides the space neatly into bar and dining areas; the floor is red-painted concrete, the tables and seating are retro café style, it's all very youthful and artistically cool. The young staff are dressed all in black and even sport specially-made Denial jewellery. The chefs are on display in an open-plan kitchen in one of the back corners; it also has bags of young, whipped-up optimism on its side.

The food is pretty hot too. Or should that be cool? Not ground-breakingly different but done very well and executed with real care for quality and generosity.

A starter of ballotine of chicken was wrapped in

pancetta, fragrant with tarragon and moistened with some excellent oil. A red pepper and goat's cheese tart was beautifully flavoured and summery and enriched with soft cheese.

Sea bass with saffron broth was an exercise in main course generosity, curled-over fillets, perfectly cooked, on a bed of white noodles and a moat of prawns, asparagus and spring onion in a stock of almost too much saffron (if such a thing were possible). A white risotto lacked a little oomph but the accompaniments - great asparagus and sunblush tomatoes and an enormous pile of pecorino - still made it a treat.

Desserts were top-notch: a chocolate tart, which hit precisely the right balance of intense chocolate and sweetness, and a lime tart made perfect by a master-stroke brulèe topping. Denial has already given itself something to live up to.

Fish! Diner and Bar

156-158 Wharfside Street,
the Mailbox, B1 1RQ. 0121 632 1212.
Website: www.fishdiner.co.uk

Fish and seafood
Mon-Sat 11.30-11.
Sun 12-10.30.
CC (closed slips).
Wheelchair access (+WC).
A/C.
1 V

Starters £3.95-5.95.

Mains £8.50-£15.

Desserts £3.95.

This is, of course, the obvious restaurant to occupy a waterside spot in the brave new world of the Mailbox.

Simplicity is at the core of Fish! Not only does it specialise in the obvious, it stakes its reputation on freshness, healthiness and choice - the choices being mainly piscine, naturally, although there are one or two things for the meatophiles and veggies who get dragged along.

Just pick which fish you want, choose the way you want it cooked - grilled or steamed - and select a sauce. And that's it. Easy peasy lemon squeezy. The fish is the star and is allowed to shine.

The decor is equally down-to-earth although in a slightly whimsical way. Someone has had fun designing a trendy version of the fish and chips caff (the word ironic was probably used), so there are chrome holders for paper napkins and sachets of ketchup and vinegar. The tables are bare, with the paper menus doubling up as mats and the chairs aren't exactly comfy.

The open plan kitchen is a mistake in a fish restaurant, unless you're very fond of the smell. Families are more than welcome and children generally love it. Service is almost as young and also eager to please - it also costs a discretionary 10 per cent on your bill.

Henry Wong

283 High Street, Harborne, B17 9QH.
0121 427 7666. Fax 0121 427 9799.

A popular feature of well-heeled Harborne's restaurant scene for many years, Henry Wong now has a trendily-refurbished interior, all smart black chairs and tablecloths, palms and metallic-effect mirrors.

Cantonese

Every day
12-2, 6-11.30.

CC
(slips left open).
Wheelchair access.
10 V.

Starters
£2.70-£14.

Mains
£6-£9.50.

Desserts
£2.30-£6.00.

Set menus
£13.50-£14.

There's more space than you'd expect behind the converted bank façade, with two connecting rooms and a small bar. But they manage to fill it all regularly thanks to a large menu that covers the expected territory reliably well.

Duck broth was a winning starter, rich with shredded meat and darkly savoury while chicken with green peppers in black bean sauce was so moreish that little of the generous portion could be abandoned. Fried aubergine in black bean sauce was also highly-seasoned and delicious but the winning vegetarian main course was sizzling wuntuns, lovely golden dumplings nicely spicy with ginger and spring onions. Rice and noodles were also more than up to the mark.

"You are just a 'girly' who must have been completely overwhelmed by the surroundings" -
Letter to Alison Davison

Service is friendly and efficient.

Birmingham

Hotel du Vin bistro ★

25 Church Street, Birmingham B3 2NR.
0121 236 0559. Fax 0121 236 0889.
Email: info@birmingham.hotelduvin.com
Website: www.hotelduvin.com

Eclectic
Every day
12-1.45, 6-10.

2 V.
CC
(slips left open).
Wheelchair access
(+WC).
Organic/
free range.

Starters
£4.50-£7.

Mains
£10.50-£16.

Desserts
£5.75.

Set Sun L
£22.50

A thoroughly French affair here with a romantic, candlelit restaurant at the heart of this utterly chic hotel which made such magnificent and thoughtful use of the old eye hospital building in the city's suits quarter.

There's no music, which may disappoint Charles Aznavour fans, but it's already attracting enough of a following to maintain a useful background buzz.

The menu is pretty well second fiddle to the wine list. The vinuous theme extends from the encyclopaedic list to the decor, with cleverly aged walls decorated with wine paraphernalia and windows full of some truly stupendous - but tragically empty - bottles.

Lots of choice (11 starters and 13 mains) covers all the basic French bistro bases with invention and a little fusion flair: A terrine of red mullet escabeche, duck confit with ratte potatoes and beetroot dressing, and citrus beurre blanc alongside the gravadlax and cucumber.

Expect a lot of fish and a healthy gallic respect for offal and bunny. Saucing is classically simple - a samphire sauce vierge makes roasted red mullet special - and luxury ingredients pop up in a decadently oily dish of pasta with wild mushrooms and truffle.

Service is eager to please and predominantly French.

> "*A man cannot make him laugh; but that's no marvel – he drinks no wine*" – Shakespeare
> (Henry IV, II)

40

Hyatt Regency Hotel ★

Court Café, 2 Bridge Street, B1 2JZ.
0121 643 1234. Fax 0121 643 2323.
Email: hrbirm@hrb.co.uk.
Website: www.birmingham.hyatt.com

Modern European
Every day
6.30-10,
12-2,
5.30-10.30.

CC.
Wheelchair access
(+WC).
A/C.
Free range, local.

Starters
£4.75-£10.75.

Mains
£7.45-£15.75.

Desserts
£4.50-£6.

Table d'hote
£11.50 - 2 courses,
£13.50 - 2 courses.

Top chef Roger Narbett is now concentrating on his venture at the Bell and Cross in Clent (see entry below) but until recently, he was the brains behind the food operation here (he also cooks for the England football team but don't hold that against him).

So you'd expect the food to hit the high spots and it doesn't disappoint. The Narbett wizardry lives on in magical concoctions of eastern spicing and traditional British and European dishes. An oriental salad and sweet chilli tamarind dressing put seared Scottish salmon high on the must-try list of starters.

A lunchtime goat's cheese main course for vegetarians is deep-fried in a delicious beignet, coloured bright yellow and lightened with turmeric.

Evening fare tends to be even more defiantly oriental with perhaps Indian-spiced chicken with Caesar salad and steamed Chinese dumplings or a Thai main course, like spiced rice noodles with vegetables, prawns and chicken.

But you don't have to be such a globe-trotter to enjoy an excellent meal. The soups are souperb (and served in temptingly-generous terrines), testosterone-loaded meat dishes abound while fish gets masses of flavour both from its sauces as well as accompaniments such as spiced gnocchi. Leave room for dessert - these are heavenly.

The great food will hopefully distract you from the international-hotel look of your surroundings. The café feels rather too much a part of the foyer and although its splendid atrium and trees give a rather grand feel, it can't give it much intimacy. Still, it does at least give you a decent amount of space between the tables - something which seems increasingly rare these days.

Indi

Ladywell Walk, Arcadian Centre,
Hurst Street, B5 4ST.
0121 622 4858. Fax 0121 622 4876.

Asian/
Mediterranean
fusion

Mon-Thurs
12-12.

Fri/Sat
12-2am.

Sun
4-10.30.

CC
(no Amex;
slips closed).
Wheelchair access
(+WC)
A/C.
8 V.

Tapas
£3.50-£4.95.

Paellas
£7.95-£9.95.

Desserts
£3.50-£4.95.

Set menus for
group bookings
£9.95-£30.

Indian tapas is the new idea here and a futuristic
interior has been designed to match it. A pre-
dinner or pre-club venue (to appeal to families as
well as the trendy city youth) is its basic aim but
presumably the dance floor will sort the family
men from the boys.

The feeling of space is utilised to the full, while
furniture is kept to a minimum. Walls are sparkling
white and dining is on refectory-style long tables
and bench seating.

The most startling section is a circular area of
sunken seating with scatter cushions 'rather like
sitting in a dry jacuzzi'.

The food is not just based on the Indian
sub-continent and Spain but runs the gamut
of Asian (including Chinese and Japanese)
and Mediterranean flavours (Italian ones
especially welcome).

It all adds up to interesting food that hits the spot.
Tapas choices include aloo gratinado (spiced
potatoes and cheese in a white wine sauce),
goshi brocheta (skewered seasoned lamb and
veg) and gambas lasan (prawns fried with garlic
and spices).

Paellas feature heavily in main course options,
along with parrillada gosht (a mixed grill of
chicken, lamb and prawn
mixed grill) and murgh
tallarines (chicken, pork
or beef with vegetable
noodles).

> **"I and many of my
> friends would like to read an article
> written by a non-vegetarian writer. One of
> your writers even had the cheek to ask for
> amuse-bouches which are 'veggie-
> friendly'!"** - Letter to The
> Birmingham Post

The Jam House

3-5 St Paul's Square, Hockley, B3 1QU.
0121 200 3030. Fax 0121 200 3044.
Email: info@thejamhouse.com
Website: www.thejamhouse.com

Fusion
Mon/Tues
12-12.

Wed-Fri
12-2am.

Sat
6pm-2am.

CC
(no Diners;
slips closed).
A/C.
Wheelchair access
(+WC, stairlift).
4 V.

L average
£5.95.

D
£20 - 2 courses,
£23 - 3 courses.

Live music comes first here - and not surprisingly, in this Jools Holland-backed venture - but the food isn't too far behind. It's a great fun venue. The knocked-through space has left enough room for a grand piano and performance space and the seating on two levels allows for plenty of tables as well as room for standing and/or bopping.

You might be feeling too old for a nightclub (this is a sentiment that strikes women of a certain age but strangely, not their male contemporaries) but you can always come here when you want to let your hair down. It has exactly the right atmosphere of easy, devil-may-care friendliness. With booze.

The menu offers world food to go with the world music. As with the music, you may not like all of it but its heart is in the right place.

Jyoti

569-571 Stratford Road, Sparkhill, B11 4LS.
0121 766 7199

South Indian
vegetarian/vegan
Tues/Wed
6-9.30.

Thurs/Fri
12-2, 6-9.30.

Sat
1-9.30.

Sun
1-8.45.

CC
(no Amex or Diners).
Wheelchair access.
A/C.

Starters
£2-£3.

Mains
6-£9.

Desserts
£2-£3.50.

Set menus available
for groups.

Vegetarian restaurants are rather thin on the ground these days but an Indian veggie restaurant has even more rarity value. Its appeal, though, now that meat-eaters don't run screaming at the thought of a non-flesh-based meal, is pretty widespread. Yes, you can bring carnivores along here and they really won't be able to complain about lack of choice or flavour.

With 22 starters and 65 main courses, this is a vegetarian heaven. It's unlicensed too which makes it a bargain - on top of the fact that starters only cost £1 to £2.65 and main courses from £2.10 to £4.45.

Nothing to break the bank then but plenty of unusual ingredients to stop you in your tracks. What exactly are colocassia leaves? What are idli, sev and shrikhand?

It's certainly worth going to find out. The array of flavours, with recurrent themes of tamarind, pulses and 'fluffy breads' were a revelation. Starters of mixed bhaji and pani puri were gutsy and satisfying. Main course selections were more hit and miss but still fantastic value.

Karibunis

South Birmingham College, Stratford Road/ Colebank Road, Hall Green, B28 8ES. 0121 694 5069. Fax 0121 694 6290. Email: stuarts@sbirmc.ac.uk

World cuisine.
Term-time only
Tues-Fri
12-2.30.
Thurs
6-9.45.
CC
(slips closed).
Wheelchair access
(+WC).
Free range/organic.
4 V.
Starters
90p-£1.75.
Mains
£3-£5.50.
Desserts
£1.25-£1.75.

If you're on the hunt for cheap food, forget the fast food joint and try Karibunis, especially on a Friday lunchtime when there's a two-for-the-price-of-one deal.

This is the restaurant arm of the college's chefs' training centre based at South Birmingham College, which encourages keen amateurs with evening courses as well as setting would-be chefs on their way with GNVQs.

Eating here is always cheap. The small menu changes fortnightly but starters cost about £1 and main courses are £3. Puddings are £1.25 and tea and coffee 50p.

Forget any ideas of stylish surroundings; the 80s-style border and multi-patterned decor, complete with speckledy industrial carpet tiles is best forgotten. And kindness is required when faced with nervous young staff.

Just tuck into surprisingly good delights like fresh, piquant vegetable pakoras or pale and creamy cauliflower soup.

Some dishes might look rather sad (blackened turkey breast steak, maybe, or tagliatelle with mushrooms) and show signs of having been plated up for a while but are still good considering what little money they cost. You can bet the pasta will be homemade and the portions will be generous.

Las Iguanas

Arcadian Centre, Hurst Street, B5 4TB.
0121 622 4466. Fax 0121 622 1378.

OK, so you don't come here for a sophisticated culinary blowout but you could do far worse when you just want a relaxed good time, perhaps with the children on a weekend lunchtime when the mood is particularly laidback (like the great salsa background music).

The food is standard Tex Mex - enchiladas, quesadillas and so on - all those wrap-type things that, as Billy Connolly once said, are really all the same thing folded different ways.

Still, it's filling enough, it won't break the bank, the service is young and friendly and the refried beans aren't anything like as bad as they sound.

Latin American
Mon-Thurs 12-11pm.
Fri/Sat 12-11.30pm.
Sun 12-10.30pm.
CC (slips left open).
Wheelchair access
(+WC).
A/C.
5 V.

Starters
£3.50-£5.

Mains
£7-£10.50.

Desserts
£3.50-£4.50.

Also meal for 2 -
£13.50 and set
menus for groups,
£14.50.

Leftbank

79 Broad Street, city centre, B15 1QA.
0121 643 4464. Fax 0121 643 5793.

As we were going to press, Leftbank was closing for a complete makeover and change of direction. After endless public confusion with Bank at nearby Brindleyplace, there was to be a new name too for its reopening with a predominantly Italian flavour in September 2001.

But as it will be led by the same team, one thing that can be relied on is its good quality. And as this is one of Birmingham's rare city centre restaurants where the tables aren't jammed too closely together and the room doesn't resemble an aircraft hangar, it should hopefully remain one of the few romantic places to go for a meal.

Lime and Chilli House ★

25 Woodbridge Road, Moseley, B13 8EH.
0121 449 4498.

Not just a funky little restaurant but also a juice/fizz bar, the Lime and Chilli has become a must-visit venue for Moseley and the surrounding suburbs. Why, even ladies from Edgbaston brave deepest bohemia (Moseley in the original Brum translates into 'land of teachers and old hippies') for a table here.

The decor matches the name so be warned - expect chilli red walls and outrageously lime woodwork. Not yer average fine dining eaterie then but certainly one which wins fans for the sheer warmth of the service. The eagerness to please is such that you can even put in a request for a special dish (within reason and 24 hours' notice) and the staff may also pop to the off licence next door to get your beer if they've got the time. (It's a bring your own with a £2 corkage charge - although this is a one-off charge for the table and not per bottle).

Customers who don't want to dream up their own menu might well find the standard one more than acceptable. Lamb cutlets with onion sauce on diced celeriac, spicy roasted Med veg on a dark aniseed sauce and oven-roasted haddock on spinach are typical of the simple yet flavoursome dishes to be had. The eponymous lime and chilli may well flavour some butter for jumbo prawns or a dip for fresh blinis. Big tasty salads also win praise.

Portions are seriously generous.

Modern British
Tues-Sat
11-3,
6.30-10.30.
Sun
11-2.30.
CC
(no Diners;
slips left open).
Wheelchair access
(+WC).
2 V.
Organic on request.
Starters
£1.75-£4.95
Mains
£9.95-£14.95
Desserts
£3.95

Maharaja

23-25 Hurst Street, city centre. B5 4AS.
0121 622 2641. Fax 0121 622 4021.

North Indian
Mon-Sat
12-2, 6-11.

The Maharaja prides itself very much on its quality reputation and serves up a favourite roll call of north Indian dishes to a fond and regular clientele. The surroundings are traditional, the staff attentive and knowledgeable.

Vegetarians are, of course, quite spoilt for choice, their options here including the exotic KK Mattar (lotus roots with peas) alongside the more usual suspects.

The kitchen shows a light touch; even dishes like the delicious starter paneer pakora - deep-fried, batter-covered chunks of spiced cheese - are remarkably non-greasy.

Classics, such as lamb rogan josh, are routinely praised for their restraint on the chilli while piling on rich flavours of spices and nuts. Freshness makes a success of the vegetable dishes too and the care taken across the board ensures the supporting roles like the rice and naan breads don't let the main players down. Expect some rather grand service.

The most favoured customers eat upstairs.

C.C.
Wheelchair access (+WC).
A/C.

Starters
£2.45-£4.05.

Mains
£7-£8.45.

Desserts
£1.70-£1.95.

Malabar

103-105 High Street, Harborne. B17 9NR.
0121 428 4466/428 4499.

A little gem for one of Birmingham's well-to-do suburbs, Malabar is a 'contemporary' Indian restaurant but it has the sense to keep all its options covered when it comes to the traditional stuff too.

So in nicely modern surroundings of pale jade and lemon walls, it sets out its stall - an appealing mix of authenticity and aspiration - very attractively indeed. It sings the praises of Malabari life (in the coastal and tropical north-east corner of Bharat), it lists lots of dishes many Indian restaurant regulars will never have heard of and it puts a whole list of champagnes on the front cover of its wine list.

But it also offers 'traditional, popular and balti' dishes with a list of curry treatments - from madras

Contemporary
Indian/Thai

Every day
5.30-11.30.

CC
(no Amex, Diners;
slips left open).
A/C
5 V.

Starters
£3.75-£6.95.

Mains
£5.95-£11.95.

to korma - of a list of chicken, lamb, king prawns, along with tandooried versions of the aforementioned and mixed veg.

The food - even the Malabari dishes - doesn't actually seem all that different in the flesh (and there's a lot of that) from what's on offer with a more standard menu but they are done very well with a palpable feeling of effort and quality. The rice was delicious too.

Vegetarians must make do with traditional treatments of mixed veg or - and this was particularly good - get a collection of some of the side vegetables, such as spinach, a 'renowned' dhal and a lovely, oily aubergine concoction.

But the best thing - and here I think they must be doing battle with their unlicensed Indian competitors - is a wine list which shows scarcely any mark-up at all. There's no need to bring your own with prices as low as these.

Marriott Hotel ★

12 Hagley Road, Five Ways,
Birmingham, B16 8SJ.
0121 452 1144. Fax: 0121 456 3442.
Website: www.marriotthotels.com/bhxbh

Both of the Marriott's restaurants are worthy of inclusion. They are:

Langtry's ★ (Marriott Hotel)

The less formal of the grand hotel's two restaurants, Langtry's is still pretty genteel, albeit in a relaxed conservatory style, all mountains of polished greenery and tiled flooring.

Modern brasserie style.

Mon-Sat 12-2.

Every day 6-10.

It isn't cheap - but then, you surely weren't expecting it to be. An ambience of unhurried quality (it can be a little too unhurried at times) like this is bound to cost, as is the excellence of the food.

It belongs to a rather simpler, more bistro-style league than its sibling Sir Edward Elgar but is equally beyond reproach. A little travelling around the world may bring gargenelli with an array of Italian veg, jambonette of chicken with chorizo or even bubble and squeak with spinach, poached egg and hollandaise within the net of the ever-capable chef Ian Mansfield.

More contemporary flavours are here but used with restraint and balanced against classics. There's a tangible feeling of knowledge and good judgement - they hold back on portion size, which I'm all in favour of. Three smaller courses you can manage easily are so much better than two kingsize ones which leave you sprawling but so often, quantity is associated with value; it takes a confident chef not to pile up the plate.

CC
(slips closed).
Wheelchair access
(+WC).
3 V.
A/C.
Organic.

Starters
£4.50-£7.50

Mains
£12.50-£16.50

Desserts
£4.50-£6

Set L
£12.50 - 2 courses,
£16.50 - 3 courses

Sir Edward Elgar ★ (Marriott Hotel)
Phone number as above.

And just across the corridor is where the Marriott ups the ante. With huge chintzy drapes, artworks all over the walls, plush seating and even a pianist (although he didn't play any Elgar when we were there), the Sir Edward Elgar is a self-consciously grand restaurant.

Happily, the service, mostly French, is young and friendly rather than pompous, the silver domes of a previous era having given way to a more low-key approach - although still thoroughly professional.

Excellent dishes typically combine top-class ingredients with technical skill in a generally faultless display of culinary excellence. Goat's cheese ravioli may be poached in chicken bouillon for a first course, or a starter of millefeuille of citrus-marinaded salmon is equally impressive. Mains sparkle with equally labour-intensive garnishing - red mullet with saffron couscous and shellfish bourride, for instance, or sea bass filled with scallop mousseline.

Everything works reliably and presentation is first class.

Classical with modern influences

Tues-Sat
7-10pm.

Sun
12-2.30.

CC (slips closed).
Wheelchair access
(+WC).
A/C.
2 V.
Organic, free range, local.

Starters
£7.50-£10.95

Mains
£16.50-£22

Desserts
£6.25-£7

Set D
£32.50 - 3 courses.

Gewurztraminer makes a good partner for Cheddar cheese, according to one wine fan.

Metro Bar and Grill ★

73 Cornwall Street, city centre, B3 2DF.
0121 200 1911. Fax 0121 200 1611.
Website: www.metrobarandgrill.co.uk

Modern European
Mon-Fri
12-2.30, 6.30-9.30.

Sat
6.30-9.30.

CC
(no Diners;
slips left open).
Wheelchair access
(+WC).
A/C.
Free range/organic.
4 V.

Starters
£4.25-£7.25.

Mains
£9.95-£17.95.

Desserts
£5.25-£5.95.

Shiny, sleek and modern, the Metro bar is slap bang in the middle of Birmingham's suits quarter and a regular haunt for Birmingham's professional and commercial classes.

Its popularity is long-lived and understandable. With its quality food (it has a Michelin Bib Gourmand) and vibrant, lively atmosphere, the Metro feels like the place to be. It caught, and more importantly held on to, a feeling of young professional style (we won't say yuppie) and it still rides that particular wave with ease.

Certainly the long bar area with its natty seating and framed cartoons, gets incredibly busy (and smoky), particularly for after-work drinking. Some complain that later in the evening, it loses its cachet a little.

The restaurant has an airy feeling of space thanks to a sizeable atrium. It's busy most of the time with a menu that gets an overhaul every four months. Expect a riot of well-crafted, inventive combinations and new tastes.

Starters (or 'first plates') can include deep-fried squid in a spiced crust with baby spinach, tartare and potato salad or a salmon, watercress and pecorino tart. There are lots of flavours piling in - smoked haddock comes with sautéed new potato, caramelised baby onions, beetroot and a poached egg - but the balancing act is a precision one with few things out of kilter.

Mains ('second plates') continue the trend with guinea fowl supreme stuffed with mozzarella, basil and garlic confit and spiced lentils or fillet of beef with polenta croute, foie gras and onion gravy. Simple tastes but well-blended, it makes for lively eating.

Mokhams

140 Digbeth, B5 6DR. 0121 643 7375.
Email: mokhams@hotmail.com

The location isn't great - although Digbeth will improve dramatically with all the development work going on - but little Mokhams is still worth the trip.

This Kashmiri balti has nice touches which set it above the average, including a choice of cooking oils, sunflower or olive, depending on how light you like your food. But its main claim to fame is its quality.

It's friendly, unassuming and as you'd expect, the choice is wide (especially good for vegetarians) and cheap. It's also bring your own, so you can save even more.

Kashmiri balti with some western influences.

Sun-Thurs 6-12.

Fri/Sat 6-2am.

CC (no Amex, slips closed)
Wheelchair access.
Free range/organic.
51 V

Starters
average £1.50.

Mains average £5.

Desserts
average £1.80.

Set menus available
for groups

Naked Pepper ★

55/59 Newhall Street, city centre, B3 3RB.
0121 212 2511. Fax 0121 212 2533.
Email: pepper@nakedrestaurants.co.uk

One of the newest arrivals in the city has confidently and colourfully taken over the old Simply Blue site with an excellent food ethos - good ingredients kept simple.

The front part of the venue is a casual, comfortable, drinking section while further back, under a stylish atrium, the dining tables line up alongside the bar and beckon to the ravenous. A large open-plan kitchen at the back of the rather tunnel-like venue has a surprisingly large number of purple-hatted chefs turning out some very good food indeed.

Simple southern Europe.

Mon-Fri
9am-10pm.

Sat
6-10.

CC
(no Diners; slips left open).
Wheelchair access
(+WC).
A/C.
5 V.

Starters
£3-£7.

Mains
£7-£17.

Desserts
£4.

The 'naked' theme applies particularly to the 'naked board' and 'naked shellfish'. With the board, prime Scottish

"Considering . . . you must virtually eat for nothing, how you can dare to grumble about a bit of grit in a mushroom risotto is beyond comprehension" -
Letter (anonymous) to
Alison Davison

chateaubriand, T-bone or rack of Welsh lamb are offered just brushed with olive oil and fresh rosemary to be shared by two with a couple of side order veg choices. With the shellfish, it's the same treatment for lobster, scallops, jumbo prawns or rock oysters.

If you want to dress such nakedness up a little, there's a list of sauces available - or you can choose from the rest of the menu, which lists brasserie-style dishes. These may sound a little predictable - fishcakes, pasta, pizzas etc - but don't be fooled. Superb quality and spot-on cooking makes them truly special.

Lobster, shrimp and salmon fishcakes are a cut above the average and the two chunky specimens that turn up as a starter err on the generous side. They're so delicious, fresh and crisp that you may find it difficult to leave room for a main course.

A special of baby chicken cooked in garlic and herbs with leek and chive mash and a red wine jus was one main course winner - and equally generous in size. Porcini fettucini was an enormous bowlful of wonderful pasta mixed with juicy mushrooms, cherry tomatoes, buffalo mozzarella and masses of fresh herbs.

Light lunchers may be better sticking to the first-rate salads and soups. Prices aren't at all bad for the quality of produce.

"Then a sentimental passion of a vegetable fashion must excite your languid spleen" – WS Gilbert

Le Petit Blanc ★

2-3 Oozells Square, 9 Brindleyplace, B1 2HS.
0121 633 7333. Fax 0121 633 7444.
Website: www.petit-blanc.com

Arty, streamlined and pure, blissful white,
Birmingham's Le Petit Blanc has been a winner
ever since it opened its beautiful doors in 1999.
The recipe is a perfect one – delicious, honest
food, full of free range integrity, which is as
comforting as it is stylish, a rare combination.

The menu offers plenty of choice and prices
are more than reasonable for such well-crafted
dishes of reliable quality. Contemporary
Mediterranean flavours may include great soups,
pasta and some exquisite risottos. I still go all
misty-eyed remembering a pumpkin risotto that
was utterly sublime, a sunset dish of creamy,
cheesy, orange heaven.

But for those who want something more rustically
French, there are the menu classics such as braised
pig's cheek and Maman Blanc pudding.

Portions are perfect, veg are extra, wines are fine
and the surroundings are beautiful. There's even a
terrace where you can admire the Brindleyplace
arty bits.

It's also the perfect feelgood place to take children
– here they are warmly welcomed rather than
tolerated and their menu, while sensibly simple,
doesn't have a chicken nugget in sight, hurrah.
The use of salt and sugar is restrained. Service is
young, utterly professional and smiley with it.

Le Petit Blanc has become a marker for quality in
the city and, at the time of going to press, was one
of only two bearers of a Michelin award – a Bib
Gourmand which applauds 'good food at
moderate prices'. (The Metro Bar and Grill in
Cornwall Street is the other, see separate entry.)

Classic French with contemporary Mediterranean

Mon-Sat 12-11.30.

Sun 12-10.30.

CC (slips left open). Wheelchair access (+WC). Organic/free range. 6 V.

Starters £4.50-£6.95.

Mains £8.25-£15.75.

Desserts £4.25-£5.25.

Set menus available.

Pizza Express

4 The Citadel, Corporation Street,
0121 236 0221.
The Water's Edge, Brindleyplace,
0121 643 2500.
153-155 High Street, Harborne,
0121 427 6009.

Also at

5 Birmingham Road, Sutton Coldfield,
0121 354 9261.
10 Hay Lane, Coventry,
0247 663356.
and 74 High Street, Stourbridge,
01384 379358.

*For Brindleyplace
(other branches
may vary):*

Traditional Italian

*Mon-Sat
1130-12 midnight*

*Sun
11.30-11.30.*

*CC
(slips left open).
Wheelchair access
(+WC).
A/C.
8 V.*

*Starters
£1.70-£3.85.*

*Mains
£4.95-£7.80.*

*Desserts
£2.10-£3.90.*

A chain that now seems to be spreading all over
the place but still a pizza paradise. Perhaps it's the
stylish surroundings - after all, not many places
offering main courses this cheap even attempt an
artistic ambience but Pizza Express, god bless 'em,
clearly felt good food deserved a good decor
whether it was pizza for the people or the foie
gras fare of fine dining.

What you get then, is a well-designed interior,
very arty (nice modern stuff on the walls), there
may even be live music (often with a jazz bent)
just to reinforce that sense of real laidback style.
It's simple - plain white spotlit walls don't actually
need much to look good but there's a knack to
making the most of minimal and black marble is
the contrast of choice in many Pizza Express outlets.

The pizzas (oh yes, the food!) are excellent. They
may have shrunk noticeably over the years but a
fiorentina with a glass of that soft house red still
adds up to heaven for me. Toppings have got
reasonably varied but they're sensible enough to
stick to a tried and tested selection. The couple
of pasta dishes are fine but not in the same
league. Likewise, puds and salads are OK without
rocking any boats.

Primitivo

10-12 Barwick Street, city centre, B3 2NT.
0121 236 6866.

Deep in Birmingham's commercial sector, Primitivo cuts its cloth to fit its professional and predominantly male clientele. Not just with an arty interior, bijou trendy bar or easy eating food but also with a surfeit of young female staff.

It's friendly, of course, and lunchtimes and after-work find the place doing exceptionally well although things quieten down noticeably mid-evening onwards. Background music has to cope with the ringing of mobile phones.

Food is mainly Mediterranean based with reasonable pasta dishes, good fish and competently-cooked meat.

International
Mon
12-3.
Tues-Fri
12-3, 6-9.
CC.
Wheelchair access
(+WC).
4 V.
Starters
£3.75-£4.50.
Mains
£6.75-£14.
Desserts
£3.50-£4.

Quo Vadis

190 Corporation Street, B4 6QD.
0121 236 4009. Fax 0121 212 0271.

Those wishing to bag themselves a lawyer (but do please try counselling first) could do worse than to hang out here in this haunt of the city's legal eagles. It is slap bang in the middle of the courts quarter and in an impressive old building of its own, if not in the ornate mould of the magistrates' court opposite.

The sizeable wine bar is of a traditional appearance - lots of dark wood, trestle-style tables, stripped floors with dark green walls - a tasteful mix of clubby colours and a nice relaxed bar style. There are newspapers to read.

Quo Vadis is a rather rare example of an individually-run place not ruined by being taken over by a big brewery. The food options, all chalked up on a blackboard, are interesting and generally done well.

Modern European
Mon-Fri
12-8.
CC.
Wheelchair access
(+WC).
A/C.
Tapas
3 for £5.
Mains
£4.75-£8.50.
Desserts
£2.50-£3.95

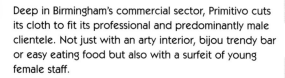

The woman in the Indian restaurant had complained that the mulligatawny soup wasn't authentic so the waiter returned from the kitchen with the proof – the empty Heinz tin – eating out in 80s Birmingham

Lots of tapas may hit the spot, fish dishes are cooked properly and usually with nice garnishes, there are equally tasty vegetarian and meaty dishes.

Some puds may look microwaved but the wine is OK, a little pricy perhaps (which is what you'd expect) but at least there's a decent variety.

Quod ★

245 Broad Street, B1 2HQ.
0121 643 6744. Fax 0121 643 6799.
Email: scoop@quod.co.uk

Italian-influenced
Every day
12-11.
CC.
13 V.
A/C.
Wheelchair access.
Starters
£3.85-£6.75.
Mains
£4.85-£13.95.
Desserts
£4.55.
Set menus, inc V,
on request.

There are so many venues on Broad Street but so few with any real appeal for the foodie (or indeed anyone over 21). Quod, a citadel to modern Italian food, is one of the rare places which have stopped it from turning into lager mile.

It does have certain characteristics in common with some of its neighbours though - it's enormous, it has a bar as well as a dining area and it is relentlessly modern. The motif here is huge photograph-based works covering at least some of the walls.

It all makes one think that most of Birmingham's youths are now employed in the service or catering trades. Here, the service was friendly enough, if a bit rough and ready; but the food, most importantly, was excellent - there was good bread to dip into olive oil while perusing a main menu with excellent pasta, gnocchi, steaks and fish (plus pizzas) or wondering whether to experiment with the specials of the day.

Everything I've come across so far has been excellent, with a genuine Italian knack of letting the flavours of great ingredients speak for themselves without too much mucking about. Delicious food, beautifully and knowledgeably cooked.

"Give me neither poverty nor riches; feed me with food convenient for me" – the Bible

Rajdoot Tandoori

12-22 Albert Street, city centre, B4 7UD.
0121 643 8805. Fax 0121 643 8749.
Website: www.rajdoot.co.uk

Rajdoot claims a place not just in Birmingham's restaurant heritage but the country's - it's said that they were the first to introduce tandoori cooking into the UK back in 1966.

There are now sibling Rajdoots in Manchester, Bristol, Dublin and even Spain but the Brum grandaddy keeps its head held high. In the large, traditional interior, the tandoor specialities (such as chicken - whether plain, chilli or rashmi) are as popular as ever but fish Amritsari (spicily-battered cod in a garlicky tomato sauce) and lamb Punjabi are also regulars in a lengthy list of favourites.

North Indian
Every day
12-2, 6.30-11.15.

A/C.
CC.
Wheelchair access.
11 V.

Starters
£3.40-£7.40

Mains
£6.95-£13.

Desserts
£2-£2.50.

Set menus
L
£7.95;
others
£14-£19.95.

Rogans

12 College Road,
Handsworth Wood, B20 2HX.
0121 515 3906.
Website: www.rogans.co.uk

The neighbourhood-caff style Rogans is a vegetarian eatery and has no airs and graces but a simple message of 'healthy food, healthy body, healthy mind'.

With its homely decor and little tables, it's just as easy to pop in for tea and homemade cake as it is to snack on various veggie burgers or fill up on patés, flans and tasty salads.

Local papers are available (not that it's Birmingham Post territory so much) and the sensible range of dishes is available to eat in or take out. Homemade falafel, cashew nut paté, chick pea and potato crumble or a mushroom stroganoff are among the veggie standards which may well make an appearance. Slightly weighty fare perhaps but there's absolutely no criticism for being down to earth rather than haute cuisine. Unlicensed and no corkage charge.

Vegetarian/vegan
Mon-Sat
12-2,
5.30-8

Organic.

Starters
£1.70.

Mains
(L)
£1.10-£3.95,
(D)
£4.25-£4.95.

Desserts
£1.50-£1.95.

Ronnie Scott's Front Room

258 Broad Street, city centre, B1 2HF.
0121 643 4525. Fax 0121 643 8086.
Email: info@ronniescotts.demon.co.uk
www.bigbearmusic.com/ronniescotts

Fusion

Mon-Sat
12-3, 7-2am.

Sun
12-3, 7-10.30.

CC
(slips left open).
Wheelchair access
(+WC).
A/C.
2 V.

L
£13.50 - 2 courses,
£15.50 - 3 courses.

D
£22.95 - 2 course,
£27.95 - 3 courses.

The Front Room at Ronnie's wants to be a little bit different from all the other bars on Broad Street - a bit more laidback, a bit more big easy. It manages pretty well too, with its low-slung squashy sofas and coffee tables and relaxed staff. Hot latino colours stop it from getting too sleepy.

But the food isn't just an afterthought to soak up foreign bottled lagers. There's an American influence thanks to Arizona-born chef Ron Jackson, who is also half-native American and half-Italian.

No surprise then that the menu is a bit of a melting pot where fusion rules.

Some of it may sound gimmicky or even downright odd but it's worth sampling; it can be surprisingly tasty and satisfying and sound technical skills are in evidence, particularly with meat and fish dishes.

Ruby Cantonese

Barnsley Road, Edgbaston B17 8ED.
0121 429 8805. Fax: 0121 429 8805.

Cantonese and
Chinese

Every day
12-2, 6-11.30.

CC
(no Diners;
slips closed).
Wheelchair access
(+WC).
A/C.
16 V.

Starters
£2.50-£5.50.

Mains
£6.45-£24.95.

Desserts
£1.95-£3.95.

Set menus available.

A solidly good neighbourhood Chinese restaurant, Ruby is also friendlier than many and well deserves its loyal local following.

The warm, brightly-lit room has a huge, red pan-tiled pretend pagoda roof along one wall and an army of bustling staff. A view of the kitchen also allows sightings of the many chefs needed to cope with the heavyweight volume which is the menu.

As well as all the set menu selections, there are more than 20 dim sum starters and a mass of main courses. Lots of sweet and sours, lots of sizzling, lots of satay and, 'seafood exclusives' all jostle for space.

Quality is mostly good, though inevitably perhaps, some dishes score more highly than others. Spring rolls and a vegetarian yuk sung were a little disappointing but a meaty yuk sung was a success, as was sizzling monkfish with ginger, tofu and mixed veg and sweet and sour chicken. Masses of punchy flavour and generous portions were high points, as was the charming and efficient service.

Saint Pauls bar and restaurant

50-54 St Paul's Square, Hockley B3 1QS.
0121 605 1001. Fax: 0121 605 0547

The look is archetypal wine bar - stripped floors and tables, a bit of bare brick, some lively colours here and there - and it's been a winner for Saint Paul's for years now.

Brunch - one Americanisation I'm all in favour of - has now been added to their rota of meal times. Otherwise, it's lunch and dinners as usual with a tempting list of bistro stuff. It mostly hits the mark and pricing is sensible.

It's a small place but it feels good. When the going gets tough and busy, the hungry get downstairs or perhaps even to an outside table if the weather's OK. Sunny days feel good in this green and pleasant part of the city. The front windows are opened up to the view of the leafy square and church and give the place almost an al fresco feel. After-work drinkers from nearby offices love it.

Modern British

Mon-Sat
12-2.30, 6-10.

Sun
12-6.

CC
(slips left open).
A/C.
2 V.

Starters
£3-£4.

Mains
£8-£14.

Desserts
£4.

"One has no great hopes from Birmingham. I always think there is something direful in the sound."
- Jane Austen (Emma)

Samosa

Auchinleck Square, Five Ways. B15 1DU.
0121 643 3898.

A second vegetarian Indian restaurant in the city and, like Jyoti in Sparkhill, fantastic value for money. An all-you-can-eat buffet costs just £4.95, lunch or evening.

Ignore the interior if you can - it's a plain, squarish place which looks like it's been filled with bits and pieces inherited from various function rooms and faded hotels - a chandelier here, executive canteen-style red upholstered chairs and tables there.

But what the hell! Family-run and eager to please, Samosa offers home-cooked food of decent quality, not in the same quantity of choice as Jyoti - you get the feeling it's just mum and maybe grandma slaving over a hot stove - but the list still includes soups, pakora, samosas (of course), a selection of curries (expect spinach, chick peas, paneer), dhals, rice and breads.

Indian vegetarian

Mon-Fri
12-3, 6-10.

Sat
4-10.

Wheelchair access.
Organic.

L and D -
£4.95
all-you-can-
eat-buffet.

Santa Fe ★

178-180 Wharfside Street, The Mailbox B1 1RN.
0121 632 1250. Fax: 0121 632 1251
Email: birmingham@santafe.co.uk

One of the most appealing places in this prestigious development so far, Santa Fe has a great waterside view and a jolly nice interior too which announces its south-west American roots in style. Brightly-coloured cowboy hats become wall decorations, slightly Mexican touches abound; the look is warm, with rich-hued, wooden chunky tables topped with candles and a wackily artistic wall.

It may not be aiming at the fine dining market but it displays some of the nicer elements of that end of the restaurant world - comfortable upholstered chairs and lots of space around the tables. It's equally good for a pals' night out, a lurve-struck pig-out or a family weekend treat.

Happily, the food is a world apart from ubiquitous

Southwest USA.

Every day
12-12.

CC
(slips left open).
Wheelchair access
(+WC).
A/C.
7 V.

Starters
£2.95-£5.95.

Mains
£5.95-£12.95.

Desserts
£2.95-£4.

Set menus
available for
groups.

chain Tex Mex fodder (although Santa Fe is itself part of a mini-chain and the culinary work of chef Rocky Durham). The Mexican feel is there - quesadillas, chillies, tortilla chips, salsa and guacamole abound - but it's done very well and with spicing that is carefully handled and restrained.

The feel is quality home cooking - Rocky's pot roast is a major hit, chunks of meltingly-soft braised beef on tons of garlic mash with perfect spicing from guajillo chillies. There are enchiladas and big-hitting stuffed chillies with cornmeal crust and lots of black beans. Pasta dishes are good and tasty and everything is very well-priced, including the wine list, which features, unsurprisingly, a range of South American bottles, including an excellent Chilean sauvignon blanc.

Top ideas include two children's menus, one for teenies and one for tweenies, and the labelling of healthier eating options (symbols amazingly absent from a dessert menu which features banana compartido and brownies with canela ice cream).

Shimla Pinks

214 Broad Street, B15 1AY.
0121 633 0366. Fax 0121 643 3325.

The Indian restaurant that broke the flocked-wallpaper mould, Shimlas is still going strong several years down the line with a mid-Broad Street spot that may have seemed a little out of the way at one time but now looks positively inspired.

If you've wondered what it would feel like to have a curry in an art gallery, a visit here should tell you. Wide open spaces, huge pictures, stylish sofas - it's got the look.

Perhaps wading through the menu bores you or you're out with your friends from Indecisives Anonymous (so who chose the restaurant?), then try an executive banquet, which brings a version of their famous Sunday night buffets to your table - as much as you want from a wide range of dishes.

Modern Indian
Mon-Fri
11-3, 6-11.
Sat
6-11.30.
Sun
6-11.
CC
(slips left open).
Wheelchair access
(+WC).
A/C.
20 V.
Starters
£4.95-£7.95.
Mains
£7.95-£12.95.
Desserts
£3.95.
Set menus
£14.95, £19.95.

The food isn't as cutting edge as the decor but it usually hits the spot. Service from ultra-cool staff (don't make the mistake I did once of going dressed in black - you'll look like a waiter) has some room for improvement and tends to slow down as the place fills up. It gets very loud too.

Shogun Teppan-Yaki

Japanese
Mon-Fri
12-2.30, 6-11.
Sat
6-11.
CC
(slips left open).
Wheelchair access
(+WC).
A/C.
1 V set menu.
Starters
£3.95-£14.95.
Mains
£10.95-£17.
Desserts
£2.50-£4.50.
10 set menus
£19.50-£31.

Unit 15F, The Water's Edge,
Brindleyplace B1 2HL.
0121 643 1856. Fax: 0121 643 5563
Email: shoguntteppanyaki@btconnect.co.uk
Website: www.shogunteppanyaki.com

Food is theatre in this cool black and white Japanese eaterie with the chefs taking centre stage amid a mountain of fish and cleavers, their arena the huge steel hotplate where they cook the food in front of your table. There can be some audience participation too when egg-juggling time comes around.

Goldfish swim, rather nervously one would imagine, in a pool set in the floor and the seating is arranged around the cooking places so everyone gets a good view of the sizzling and chopping floorshow.

It's a bit like sitting in someone's kitchen wondering whether or not you should try to make conversation but it can be a fun place for groups who fancy culinary cabaret.

Sobar

Eastern
Mon-Sat
12-2am.
Sun
12-12.30am.
CC
(no Amex, Diners;
slips closed).

Arcadian Centre, Hurst Street,
city centre, B5 4TD.
0121 693 5084. Fax: 0121 693 5085.
Email: sobar@zoom.co.uk
Website: www.sobar.co.uk

Birmingham's first noodles bar, Sobar is a trendy little joint, all low brown leather seats and minimalist wooden chairs in this odd little centre off Hurst Street.

Music matters and evenings get very loud. There's a DJ set-up in a corner and a small dance floor for those who feel able to move after fry-ups like 'Japanese-style tempura vegetables' (probably carrot, courgette and onion) served with a nice, sweet, chilli sauce dip and chicken and shiitake mushrooms with pak choi and noodles in oyster sauce.

A serviceable mix of Japanese/Chinese with bitter on tap! This is one for the under-25s.

Thai Edge ★

7 Oozells Square, Brindleyplace, B1 2HL.
0121 643 3993. Fax 0121 643 3993.

Some may carp about allegedly less than authentic aspects to parts of the interior at this consummately stylish restaurant but I guess the vast majority of the diners are unlikely to get their tom yums in a twist over such matters.

After all, it looks good and it tastes good and that's pretty well all that's required for the most part.

Staff in opulent purple are wreathed in smiles and greet everyone beautifully. The place looks fabulous, from the clever little feather-strewn wall frieze (I hesitate to call it anything as naff as a dado) to the wackery screens.

As for the food, the variety is huge. Though many dishes, as is so often the case with eastern cuisines, are fried, there are interesting salads too - king prawns with lemon grass and onion or green papaya with ground peanuts, lime, garlic and tomatoes to name but two.

Fish and seafood are the key players but there are plenty of fascinating vegetable dishes either as side orders or star attractions. Some vegetarian dishes may contain nam pla (fish sauce), check first.

One wine fan insists there's only one wine to go with hot dogs – Cotes du Rhone.

Wheelchair access (+WC).
A/C.
3 V.

Starters
£3.95-£4.95.

Mains
£5.95-£6.95.

Desserts
£2.95.

Until 5pm,
2 courses - £6.95.

Thai

Mon-Thurs
12-2.30, 5.30-11.30,

Fri/Sat
5.30-12,

Sun
12-3, 5.30-11.

CC.
Wheelchair access (+WC).
A/C.
8 V.

Starters
£5.50-£7.

Mains
£7.90-£28.

Desserts
£3.50-£4.50.

Set menus
£15.50-£28.50.

Thai Mirage ★

41-43 Hurst Street, city centre, B5 4BJ.
0121 622 2287.
Email adeline@thaimirage.co.uk

Modern Thai
Sun-Thurs
12-2.30, 5.30-11.30.
Fri/Sat
12-2.30, 5-12.
CC
(slips left open).
Wheelchair access
(+WC).
A/C.
10 V.

Starters £5-£8.
Mains £7.50-£25.
Desserts £3-£4.50.
V and other set
menus
£15.50 -£25.50.

From the same team as Thai Edge, this, naturally enough, follows a similar winning theme - a beautifully modern interior and spot-on food elegantly served.

Dark wooden statues help break up the whiteness of the decor and add extra interest to the curiously-fashioned sloping walls. Windows make up practically the whole frontage so you can watch the world go by - or they can watch you.

Dishes manage to be tasty without hitting chilli overload, servings are plentiful. The crowds love it.

Tiger Tiger

Five Ways, Broad Street, B15 1DA.
0121 643 9722. Fax 0121 643 5988.
Email: info@tigertiger-birm.co.uk
Website: www.tigertiger-birm.co.uk

Modern British
Tues-Sat
5pm-2am.
CC
(slips left open).
Wheelchair access
(+WC).
A/C.
2 V.

Starters
£3.75-£9.25.

Mains
£8.75-£13.50.

Desserts
£3.50-£4.10.

Set D
£16.95 -2 courses,
£19.95 - 3 courses.

This is a warren of a place, with each of the many rooms taking on a differently-themed decor. The priority is a good time for the over-25s and the eager-to-please service reflects it. Food is important, but not that important.

So in the church-like gothic of the restaurant, there'll be lots of enjoyable dishes; they may not hit the culinary high spots but at least they're not just blotting paper for alcohol.

The basic ingredients are perfectly sound and the general impression is enjoyable, if not outstanding. The execution could be a bit sharper - chargrilled asparagus is fine, though the mozzarella with it would have worked better in a buffalo version. Tiny, spiced lamb fillets were satisfying, while a main course of spicy Portuguese chicken was simply enjoyable and a well-cooked pasta with rare duck breast worked well, even if its sauce was underwhelming. Puddings can be surprisingly good, especially a polenta cake with an intensely-orange syrup.

Tin Tin

The Water's Edge, Brindleyplace, B1 2HL.
0121 633 0888. Fax 0121 633 0868.

Chinese

Mon-Fri 12-2.10, 5.30-11.10.

Sat 12-2.10, 5.30-11.40.

Sun 12.30-3 (buffet), 3.30-10.40.

A big Chinese restaurant with a seemingly-unabating popularity, Tin Tin's first floor situation gives it a fine vantage point over the Brindleyplace crowds, although the smallish circular windows don't provide too much of a view.

At least there's a lot to see inside - it's a big place, packed with tables and diners. Luckily, the kitchen seems well able to cope, even if the waiting staff can seem overstretched and occasionally forgetful.

CC (slips left open). Wheelchair access (+WC). A/C. 15 V.

Starters £3.80-£8.40.

Mains £7.20-£9.80.

Desserts £1.95-£4.20.

Set menus £14.80-£26.80.

Traditionalists will be more than happy with a menu which offers among its notable highlights excellent chicken or king prawns with green pepper and black bean sauce and delicious satay mixed vegetables.

La Toque d'Or ★★

27 Warstone Lane, Hockley, B18 6JQ.
0121 233 3655.
E-mail: didier@latoquedor.co.uk
Website: www.latoquedor.co.uk

Classical French with a modern twist.

Tues-Fri 12.30-2.

Tues-Sat 7-9.30.

This is a rare jewel in Birmingham - a small and individually-owned restaurant with the owner slaving away in the kitchen and partner running front of house. But this is just what upwardly-mobile Hockley deserves.

CC (no Diners; slips left open). Wheelchair access (+WC). Local/free range/organic. A/C. 1 V.

And how good it is - French chef Didier Philipot, formerly of Brockencote Hall in Chaddesley Corbett (see separate entry) is a talented guy and wife Kathy leads a friendly waiting team.

L £12.50 - 2 courses, £15.50 - 3 courses;

The food is less formal and complex than his old menus for Brockencote but no worse for that - this

D £23.50 - 3 courses; some supplements.

sort of delicious simplicity is equally attractive, the quality is comparable and it costs less too.

A set menu may offer artichoke and mackerel tart with a garden herb dressing or courgette flower, chicken and chive mousse as delightful starters. Mains are superb, whether roasted quail with smoked bacon potato, truffle-scented jus, spinach and mushrooms or fillet of silver bream with a red wine emulsion and spring vegetables. There are also supplements (which can bump up the price). Exemplary cooking skills, good produce and inspired flavours make for three memorable courses. Don't expect massive servings - this is concentrated stuff to savour.

The restaurant is attractive, with bare brick walls and pretty stained glass windows but it is a bit cramped; banquette seats line the walls and the tables are rather crammed in.

The name is neatly whimsical - a reference to cooking (a toque is the tall white hat chefs wear) and the restaurant's Jewellery Quarter surroundings.

Ty's Jazz and Spice

132 Stratford Road, Sparkbrook, B11 1AJ.
0870 0660 069 (day) 0870 0660 868 (eve).
Fax: 0121 773 1632.
Website: www.tys-jazzspice.co.uk

Kashmiri
Mon-Thurs
12-2.30, 5-11.30.

Fri/Sat
5-12.

Sun
12-9.

CC
(slips left open).
Wheelchair access
(+WC).
20-25 V.

Starters
£1.50-£3.95.

Mains
£5-£11.

Desserts
£1.50-£3.

Group set menus
by request.

A Kashmiri jazz bar and restaurant - can't be many of those about, I hear you wonder. And you'd be right. Ty's is actually the only one in the UK, a fact it likes to trumpet loudly (in an improvisational sort of way). Nice.

Named after owner Ty Mamood, it's an extraordinary place all round - a converted bank, grade 2 listed and looking rather stately in cream with a smart door canopy. The interior is pretty cool too, with wooden blinds at the windows, high ceilings and stripped floor.

The performers on the restaurant stage may be

more King Pleasure and the Biscuit Boys than Miles Davis (call for details) but it makes for a fun, if very loud, evening. The food is more expensive than your average Indian restaurant but takes account of the fact that often you're getting a band thrown in.

Starters run the usual gamut from bhajis to tandoori appetisers like chicken pang and lamb chops. Mains offer a lot of simple choice within straightforward Kashmiri / jalfrezi / kofta / biriani etc sections. There's an equal amount of choice in the wide-ranging wine list.

Verde ★

27 Wharfside Street, The Mailbox, B1 1RD.
0121 632 1444. Fax 0121 632 1441.
Email: verdepeople@netscapeonline.co.uk

Ultra modern, clean and airy, Verde is the only eaterie in the Mailbox's swanky retail section, where it tempts passing shoppers and office workers with some of the best fast food around.

You can eat in (at refectory-style, pale wood tables and chairs) or take out daytime fare which is kept simple but is still vibrantly fresh and delicious. Salads, soups and panini are available, chosen in an unusual system where you pay before wandering around with your chosen plate size.

It may sound a little uninspiring but wait until you see what's on offer. Salads are gorgeously colourful and tempting, from couscous to pasta and rice via every sort of leaf; at least three soups are made daily and are divine, perhaps cumin-scented roasted veg, dished up with lovely chunks of herby Italian breads.

Two chefs man a station preparing the panini. Fillings are modern and comforting - maybe Thai chicken or tomato, basil and mozzarella. Puds are limited to pastries and moist cakes.

Feelgood food.

*Every day
10-6.*

*CC
(no Amex;
slips closed).
Wheelchair access
(+WC).
A/C.
Organic/
free range.
Large V choice.*

*Mains
£3.75-£7.*

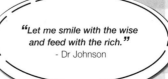

"Let me smile with the wise and feed with the rich."
- Dr Johnson

Warehouse café

54-57 Allison Street, Digbeth, B5 5TH.
0121 633 0261.

Vegetarian
Tues-Thurs
12-2.30.

Fri
12-2.30, 6-9.

Sat
12-3, 6-9.

Organic/
free range.

D Starters
£1.95-£2.55.

Mains
£7.45.

Desserts
£2.

L average
£5 - 2 courses.

The trusty Warehouse café has been a part of
Birmingham veggie life for ever and still maintains a
faithful following prepared to troop along some of
the city's less attractive streets to this hidden-away
spot down among the arches.

It's more than worth the stroll. Up in the pine-
dominated first floor caff, the food is good quality
and cheap (made by the busy Molly in the
kitchen) and served with easy friendliness. All very
right-on, of course (Friends of the Earth have their
local base downstairs) but thoroughly relaxed and
free of pretension.

It's also a comfortable place to go and eat if
you're solo. Some dishes are tried and tested
regulars (cashew nut paté and houmous, for
instance), there'll probably be curried dishes or
a flan (I tried a lovely tomato and olive version).
These come with a trio of tasty salads. And there
may also be tagines or Thai pancakes to squash
any accusations of living in the past.

It's unlicensed but there are interesting soft drinks
on offer for those who don't want to bring their own.

The café is newly-extended and now offers more
pleasantly-decorated space for its happy diners.

Wing Wah ★

278 Thimble Mill Lane,
Nechells, B7 5HD.
0121 327 7879. Fax 0121 327 7951.

Chinese
Mon-Sat
11-11.

Sun
11-10.30.

CC
(no Diners;
slips left open).

For my money, the best Chinese restaurant in
Birmingham, Wing Wah is part of the flamboyantly
oriental complex which also houses the Wing Yip
supermarket and warehouse - a big and hugely
successful bit of Chinatown not far from the
city centre.

I hesitate to trot out the old adage about how it must be good because it's full of Chinese diners - after all, do the Chinese look at McDonald's and say it must be good because it's full of English? But the evidence here seems overwhelming; it's an enormous place, always busy and always, yes, with Chinese (it's so handy when you've done your shopping next door) but by no means totally so.

Inside the traditional, functional dining room, an enormous plethora of dishes awaits to confound those bewildered by choice. Even regular diners must be confused by some of the items which turn up occasionally as specials, such as ostrich neck (they must have some very long plates) or 'fat end'.

The turnover is so fast and furious that hot, fresh food can be relied upon. Service is brisk and some rare bargains are available - including as-much-as-you-can-eat buffets, although the food in these isn't quite in the same league as the à la carte, which is fair enough.

Wheelchair access
(+WC).
A/C.
19V

Starters
£1.95-£9.

Mains
£7.20-£20.

Desserts
£1.95-£3.50.

Set menus
£12.50-£22.

Buffet
£7.50-£12.90.

Xaymaca

34 Bristol Street, B5 7AA. 0121 622 3332.
Email: xaymaca@faxvia.net
Website: www.xaymaca-experience.co.uk

Not many venues will suggest that you limbo from the bar into the restaurant but they do at Xaymaca. It is then, a bit of a party place, friendly, laidback, a little bit of Jamaica on the mean streets of Brum.

It's not an exterior you're likely to miss - small as it is, it's decorated in bright green and yellow. After the plantation-style bar at the front, the restaurant has a colourful party decor to go with the atmosphere and a large TV screen on one wall may be showing concert footage of Bob Marley tributes - an unusual way of supplying background music.

The menu offers a contemporary version of Caribbean cuisine but if traditional stuff is what you're after, it's certainly here, with goat curries and ackee and saltfish among the pepperpot soups, calaloo and plantain, cassava and yam.

Traditional
Caribbean in
a contemporary
style.

Tues-Sat
7-late.

CC
(slips left open).
Wheelchair access
(+WC).
3 V.

Starters
£3.25-£3.95.

Mains
£6.95-£8.95.

Desserts
£2.50-£3.95.

Set menus
available
for groups.

More modern touches may put filo pastry round some of those old vegetable favourites for a rather solid veggie option. As a cuisine, there's a lot of hot saucing and it's quite heavy - a lot of things are fried - but it's good fun, with the sort of feelgood factor you should be able to bottle.

BISHOPS TACHBROOK

Mallory Court ★★

Harbury Lane, Bishops Tachbrook,
Leamington Spa, Warwickshire, CV33 9QB.
01926 330214. Fax 01926 451714.
E-mail: reception@mallory.co.uk
Website: www.mallory.co.uk

French/British
Mon-Fri
12-2.30, 7-10.
Sat
12-2.30, 7-10.30.
Sun
12-2.30, 7-9.
CC
(slips closed).
Wheelchair access
(+ WC).
1 V.
Starters
£12-£35
Mains
£19-£35
Desserts
£7.50-£9.50
Set price
L
£25,
D
£37.50 (3 courses)

As if it wasn't enough having a beautiful house, in a beautiful place and with beautiful grounds, Mallory Court gets everything else right too. Young chef Steve Love is an award-winner (and a former Roux brothers' scholar) who provides exquisite food for the country house hotel's fine wood-panelled restaurant.

It's not cheap of course, but the quality is excellent and the setting divine. They've also got some great staff who manage to create an aura of ease and comfort rather than stuffy formality - a real gift.

A lovely terrace is available for outdoor dining and hotel guests are in for many luxurious treats (the hotel is a member of the prestigious Relais et Chateaux group) - there's an outdoor swimming pool, as well as tennis courts and a croquet lawn.

There are daytime snacks available and a lunch menu keeps it light and simple but very classy with three courses that may involve starting with quail and black pudding salad, going on to red mullet with shellfish sauce and finishing with passion fruit delice.

But tempting tables d'hote are rather overshadowed by a luxury-stuffed à la carte which has what must be the most expensive starter around - Oscietre caviar with blinis and crème fraiche at £35. If that's too much, there may be roast pigeon with bacon risotto or pancetta-wrapped scallops.

The motif is good ingredients not treated too fussily, with grilled Dover sole with parsley butter or canon of lamb with confit tomato and a red wine jus. Not that the grander classics are neglected - this is the place to find tournedos Rossini or lobster thermidor. High living indeed

BOURNHEATH

Nailer's Arms

62 Doctor's Hill, Bournheath, Bromsgrove, B61 9JE. 01527 873045. Fax 01527 876358. Email: info@thenailers.co.uk
Website: www.thenailersarms.com

Bournheath is a dinky little village just outside the throbbing metropolis of Bromsgrove. Its main claim to fame is as the birthplace of AE Housman (yes - I thought he was a Shropshire lad too).

It has more hostelries than it really deserves - two or three at least within staggering distance of each other - but the Nailer's Arms is the best destination for the starving.

This is a country pub with a staggeringly modern interior (think Habitat in the Woolpack), and is as splendidly ambitious in its food as its decor. The dining room is decked out in sweeping, powerful colours, blonde wood tables and artistic accessories, a spotlit modern wonder.

Dishes like Thai-spiced mussels, cumin-spiced salmon and fillet steak with herb polenta and wild mushrooms are designed to impress as well as satisfy and for the most part carry it off with some ease. Trendiness for its own sake may be suspected but happily, enough attention is paid to quality to get this turbo-charged pub grub hitting all the right buttons.

Classic/European influences.

Mon-Thurs
12-3, 6-9.30.

Fri, Sat
12-3, 6-10.

Sun
12-6.

CC
(closed slips).
A/C.
Wheelchair access
(+WC).
3V.

Starters
£3.45-£5.45.

Mains
£5.95-£15.95.

Desserts
£3.93-£6.25.

BRIMFIELD

Roebuck Inn

Brimfield, Ludlow. SY8 4NE.
01584 711230. Fax 01584 711654.
E-mail: dave@roebuckinn.demon.co.uk
Website: www.roebuckinn.co.uk

Eclectic
Mon-Sat
12-2.30, 7-9.30.

Sun
12-2.30, 7-9.

CC
(no Amex, Diners;
slips closed).
Wheelchair access.
Free range/
organic.
6 V.

Starters
£3.50-£6.25.

Mains
£7.95-£19.95.

Desserts
£4-£4.50.

Set L and D
£20 - 3 courses.

It seems rather greedy that Ludlow's fine gourmet reputation even extends to some of the village pubs in its outlying regions.

The Roebuck may be a rather inconspicuous inn but chef-owner David Wilson-Lloyd is rated sufficiently highly to be included in Ludlow's cookery demonstrations during its September food fair. An honour indeed, joining the likes of Shaun Hill and Claude Bosi.

In the beamed, cosy interior of the three bars or the sunny, contemporary dining room, a knowledgeable menu offers modern brasserie standards like duck confit as well as traditional roasts and steamed steak and mushroom suet pudding. It can be quite complex fare and also pretty big - a fillet Roebuck for instance is a chunky fillet stuffed with stilton, wrapped in bacon and served with Madeira sauce. No swimming the Channel after that.

It's a free house but the beer choice is accompanied by local ciders and perries and a wine list extensive enough to cope with the high-flying menu, including some American numbers (Firesteed Pinot Noir from Oregon to name but one). The busy, quality-minded kitchen also turns out its own breads and petit fours. Rooms available.

"I'm not really a gourmet – more of a greasy spoon man I'm afraid but my favourite restaurants are Italian - usually Valentinos in Harborne, Giovannis in Kings Heath or Pasta di Piazza in Hockley." - Nick Owen, Midlands Today

BROAD CAMPDEN

Malt House

Broad Campden, nr Chipping Campden,
Glos GL55 6UU. 01386 840295.

Yawn. Another beautiful Cotswold building,
another fantastic garden, another classy restaurant.

This one, a long, low, 16th-century limestone
malting house, is rather out of the way in Chipping
Campden's little sibling village. Serenely quiet, totally
chocolate box; green deckchairs dotted around
the four exquisite acres of enclosed, landscaped
gardens, an orchard, even a babbling brook.

To get to the restaurant, you must find your way
through a warren of exquisitely beamed and
antique-filled rooms (one decorated with gold
leaf). Then, sink into your chair and leave your
cares behind (any financial worries especially) as
you choose from the day's selection.

The tiny wine list (of about 20 bottles) was sensibly
priced and still managed to contain some little
gems - Chateau Musar from the Lebanon, Caballo
Loco Number Six from Chile, and Qupe Cabernet
Sauvignon from California - to make up for the
absence of a list of venerable Clarets and Burgundies.

It's a little hushed and very well-behaved but fans
of the English country house hotel will feel very
comfortably at home.

Modern British

Thurs-Sun
from 7.30.

CC
(slips closed).
Wheelchair access.
Organic/
free range. 1 V.

£28.50
- 3 courses.

BROADWAY

Lygon Arms (+ Olivers Brasserie) ★

High Street, Broadway, Worcs WR12 7DU.
01386 852255. Fax: 01386 858611.
Email: info@the-lygon-arms.co.uk
Website: www.savoygroup.com

Broadway is one of the must-see villages in the
Cotswolds but has nowhere near as many good
eating places as nearby Chipping Campden. What it
has got, of course, is the world-famous Lygon Arms

British with classical
French techniques

Oliver's Every day
12-2, 7-9.

*Great Hall
restaurant*

*Mon-Thurs
7.30-10am,
12.30-2, 7-9.*

*Fri/Sat
12.30-2, 7-10.*

*Sun
12.30-2.*

*CC
(slips left open).
Wheelchair access
(+WC).
Organic/
free range.
5 V.*

*Starters
£3.90-£15.50.*

*Mains
£9.50-£28.*

*Desserts
£4.25-£9.95.*

*Set menus
£36.50 (weekday);
£42.50 (Fri);
£39.50 (V).*

with its Olivers brasserie. The Lygon has been renowned for hundreds of years as a coaching inn and is considered one of the Cotswolds' finest hotels; now it appeals hugely to the American market as a typical slice of olde England.

You can eat here or in Olivers, which is in a separate building but still attached to the mother ship. The main restaurant is in an aircraft hangar of a dining room overlooking the high street.

The style of food could be called fusion but the phrase 'less is more' springs to mind all the way though the menu. Lemon grass, spearmint oil, roasted orange sauce ... there's a lot going on.

Olivers, on first appearance, seems quite austere, with dark oak furniture, subdued lighting - gentleman's club in style but with welcoming, warm staff.

The menu follows a similar pattern to the main Lygon restaurant with dishes such as tronçon of west coast salmon on roasted courgettes with sweet peppers, chilli oil and natural yogurt.

Puddings at Olivers are also lively. Spiced pear and ginger crumble with chocolate sauce and banana ice cream sounded a bit heavy but vanilla panna cotta with prunes steeped in Earl Grey tea hit the mark.

BROMSGROVE

Grafton Manor ★

Grafton Lane, Bromsgrove, Worcs, B61 7HA.
01527 579007. Fax: 01527 575221.
Email: steven@graftonmanor.u-net.com
Website: www.graftonmanorhotel.co.uk

*Modern British with
Indian influences*

*Sun-Fri
12.30-1.30.*

*Mon-Sat
7.30-9.30.*

You have to fit in around wedding parties when you want to dine at Grafton Manor these days but it's still worth the effort.

The setting is wonderful - a grand 16th century building (although largely rebuilt in the 18th century) with its own chapel and grounds, the space of some of which is pressed into use for produce for the hotel's kitchens.

The place is family-run and chef Simon Morris (son of the owner) is a renowned Indiaphile, whose eastern influences colour the menu and also lead to a feast of Indian cooking in the early part of each year. (He has also won various curry chef awards).

So, among the stolidly upper class English/French fare, expect to see, for example, some very good Bombay prawns, perhaps with a trio of sauces (all Empire-led) or some delicious Goan bread rolls to help the starters along.

Vegetarians will get their own menu with at least three flavour-packed choices at each course. Puddings are excellent; look out for a superb rice pudding with coconut or lemon posset or a sumptuous chocolate tart.

Service can be young and inexperienced but the surroundings are mellow enough to keep diners sufficiently relaxed.

CC
(slips closed).
Organic/
free range. 3 V.

L
£20.50 – 3 courses.

D
£27.85 – 3 courses,
£32.75 – 4 courses.

Sun L
£18.50 – 3 courses.

BUCKLAND

Buckland Manor ★

Buckland, near Broadway, Worcs. WR12 7LY.
01386 852626. Fax 01386 853557.
Email: enquire@bucklandmanor.com
Website: www.bucklandmanor.com

A friend said this was just the sort of place he'd take a new girlfriend to impress her. Actually, he used a much earthier phrase I wouldn't distress you with here.

Don't worry about the thought of such low-brow company spoiling your visit though. Everyone will be on their best behaviour in this gorgeous little pearl of Cotswold fine dining and country housing.

Electric gates let you into the grounds, then it's along the tree-lined gravel drive up to the entrance where you'll be greeted as an old family friend. Good-sized aperitifs are a sensible idea

British with
French influences.

Every day
12.30-1.45, 7.30-9.

CC
(slips left open).
Wheelchair access.
2 V.

Starters from £7.

Mains
£6.50-£15.25.

Desserts
£8.75-£9.

Set L
£28.50,

D
£45.50 – 3 courses.

(whether by the fire in winter or out in the garden in summer) when pondering the menu and enormous wine list.

It's serious, sophisticated fare but right on the button - fresh, simply cooked fish, game when in season, the best beef - beautifully presented and executed. When three courses cost £45.50, it's only right to expect marinated figs and cherries with your poached duck foie gras or a langoustine mousse stuffing and vanilla-flavoured langoustine bisque with a fillet of lemon sole. Leave room for a delicious pud or the great cheeseboard.

Buckland is a Relais et Chateaux hotel so it has all the luxury paraphernalia you'd expect, croquet lawn and swimming pool included. It can be intimidating but treat it with respect, your best clothes, five hours of your time (it should never be rushed) and a flexible wallet and you're in for a memorable occasion.

CHADDESLEY CORBETT

Brockencote Hall ★

Chaddesley Corbett, Kidderminster, Worcs. DY10 4PY. 01562 777876. Fax 01562 777872. email: info@brockencotehall.com Website: www.brockencotehall.com"

Modern French
Sun-Fri
12-1.30, 7-9.30.

Sat
7-9.30.

CC (slips closed.
Wheelchair access
(+WC).
3 V.

Starters
£5.50-£13.50

Mains
£13.50-£22.50.

Desserts
£5.30-£8.50.

Set menus
L
£12 - 2 courses,
£15 - 3 courses.

Jerome Besançon is the new kid here, having taken over from Didier Philipot who went on to open his own place in Birmingham (see La Toque d'Or).

Didier's a tough act to follow but this young Frenchman seems to have a good handle on things and is presumably not overawed by his surroundings - seriously gracious though they are. The village of Chaddesley Corbett is delightful and Brockencote, despite its typically English surroundings, looks just like a French chateau. It sits regally in 70 acres of lovely Worcestershire greenness, the grounds dotted with sheep or molehills or a combination of the two.

A huge sweeping drive will eventually deliver you

Sat D
£27.50.

Sun L
£22.50 - 3 courses.

(having first passed the lake and a 'ducks crossing' warning sign) to the door, where a friendly, if rather correct, welcome awaits.

Menus can be perused, and delicious nibbles sampled, in a large conservatory. It's very spacious but the dramatically-draped ceiling is looking a little 80s and if it's sunny, it can get very hot.

Then again, so can the dining room, or rather rooms as there are several interconnecting chambers. All face south and have gloriously big windows.

The food is 'proper' French - formal restaurant fare, perfect for a serious celebration when you want to push the boat out, although it can be on the stiff side when it comes to ambience.

À la carte delights may include a lasagne of wild sea bass, aubergine caviar and chargrilled courgette in a shellfish broth or tournedos of veal in pink peppercorns with wild mushroom parmentier potato and dried Parma ham.

CHELTENHAM

Le Champignon Sauvage ★

24-26 Suffolk Road, Cheltenham, Glos, GL50 2AQ. 01242 573449. Fax 01242 254365.

Startling things go on in this rare restaurant, which boasts two Michelin stars (what an achievement - there are only nine others in the country).

With a strongly French base, the cooking displays a rare degree of concentrated effort and impressive skill. Coupled with a culinary imagination which fires on all cylinders, it makes for the sort of menu that foodies must dream about - dishes which can take a page or so and a new ink cartridge to describe.

If you want to know precisely which mushroom variety you're eating, this is the place (it is Le Champignon Sauvage after all). If you fancy roasted roe deer with Szechuan peppercorns and roast beetroot or maybe fillet of brill with pan-fried pear and celeriac, book that table now. Your meal will

Cuisine terroir – French food with innovative spicing and seasoning.

Tues-Sat
12.30-1.30,
7.30-9.

CC
(slips left open).
Wheelchair access.
24 hrs notice
for V.
Free range.

L
2 courses £16.50,
3 courses £19.95.

D
Tues-Fri
2 courses - £17.95,
3 courses - £21.50.

Tues-Sat
2 courses - £33,
3 courses - £39.

be added to with amuse-bouches, appetisers, pre-desserts, even a pre-cheese cheese.

This is food as religion, all-fascinating and all-important; a ferocious, creative energy is put into it. The Provençal-coloured interior with walls filled with original art is friendly, as is your hostess Helen Everitt-Matthias, but the approach can be dominated by high priest/chef David Everitt-Matthias.

He knows his stuff and more, that is without a doubt. But you may find the experience rather high-minded.

Le Petit Blanc ★

The Promenade, Cheltenham,
Glos, GL50 1NN.
01242 266800. Fax 01242 266801.
Email: Cheltenham@lepetitblanc.co.uk
Website: www.petit-blanc.co.uk

French with
Mediterranean
and Asian accents

Mon-Sat
11am-10.30.

Sun
11am-10pm.

CC
(slips left open).
Wheelchair access
(+WC).
A/C. Organic/
free range.
4 V.

Starters
£4.50-£6.25.

Mains
£8.25-£15.75.

Desserts
£4.75-£5.75.

Set menu
L and
Sun-Thurs 6-8,
Fri/Sat 6-7.
£12.50 - 2 courses,
£15 - 3 courses.

Within the regal splendour of the pristine Queen's Hotel, Raymond Blanc's brasserie is a young, lively upstart who gets away with its zippy modernism because, basically, it has its act together and provides excellent food in a venue that welcomes families as much as businessmen.

The look is consummately stylish with an arty food mural fencing in a spacious room filled with shiny metallic tables and divided from the kitchen by swish opaque glass doors.

Petit Blanc regulars in Birmingham will know what to expect from the menu: Regional French dishes and modern European fare beautifully cooked and served by smoothly competent staff in an operation that runs on castors. Flavours are fresh, well-combined and remarkably vibrant. Whatever your cares and worries when you arrive, a meal at Le Petit Blanc makes the world seem a better place afterwards.

CHIPPING CAMPDEN

Cotswold House Hotel ★

Hick's Brasserie, The Square,
Chipping Campden, Glos, GL55 6AN.
01386 840330. Fax 01386 840310.
Email: reception@cotswoldhouse.com
Website: www.cotswoldhouse.com

**Modern British
Every day
9.30am-10pm.
CC
(no Diners).
4 V.
Local produce.
Starters
£3.75-£6.75.
Mains
£9.50-£15.50.
Desserts
£3.95-£5.50.
Set 2-course L
£10.95.**

This elegant hotel offers traditional fine dining in its more formal restaurant at weekends but Hick's, its more relaxed sibling, is already winning legions of fans for its good food in easy surroundings both at weekends and during the week as well.

It's stylish too, of course, with all the uncluttered elegance of a modern art gallery with its spotlights and carefully chic bowls of flowers. But despite the emphasis on style, it's also comfortable, with mix-and-match checked, cloth-covered and leather chairs and soft, natural colours so warm and easy on the eye.

The food is pretty global and this may actually involve some British offerings (trendy comfort stuff like battered hake with pea purée and chips), or there'll be a glimpse westward with Jamaican grilled jerk for instance, or eastward with Thai flavourings spicing up some nicely-cooked salmon.

Med favourites tend to make up the backbone though, with fine soufflés, terrines, smoked duck and risottos alongside brasserie favourites like fishcakes and scallops.

Quality is reliable and spicing user-friendly - no nasty surprises here from the chilli jar. Garnishes are particularly inventive and work well, such as julienned celeriac and apple with cider vinaigrette on smoked duck, though traditional dishes of side veg can be superfluous.

Looking for the best fish and chips in Brum? Look no further, than Bedders on the Coventry Road, Small Heath, an aficionado claims.

Modern European

Mon-Thurs
12-2, 6.30-9.

Fri/Sat
12-2.30.

Sun
12-2.30.
(+ Sun eves
prior to bank
holidays).

CC
(no Amex, Diners;
slips left open).
Local produce.
2 V.

Starters
£3.50-£5.50.

Mains
£8.50-£16.50.

Desserts
£3.95.

Set menus on
request.

Eight Bells Inn ★

Church Street, Chipping Campden,
Glos, GL55 6JG.
01386 841669. Fax 01386 840371.
Website: www.eightbellsinn.co.uk

Ah, the Cotswolds. The church clocks standing at quarter to three and there are honey-coloured buildings where you can still take tea - and honey-coloured pubs, too, where you can get the sort of fabulous lunch or great dinner which puts our city centre hostelries to shame.

The Eight Bells is a prime example. Tucked away down one of this lovely village's many lovely streets, this 14th century building really looks the part; little mullioned windows, warm stone walls, flagstoned floors, beams - the works.

But fancy getting all this and great food! We're just not used to being spoiled this way. Fantastic soups oozing rich, creamy flavours - shouldn't they be out of some anonymous vat somewhere? A beignet of goat's cheese on tomato and onion compote or slow-roasted breast of lamb on rosemary pesto - shouldn't these be out of a freezer and cooked to soggy extinction in a microwave?

It's tough - and believe me, I know - not to taste such miracles and not feel a teensy bit outraged that so many pubs employ surly spotty youths to dish up production line pap and expect you to pay happily for the honour of narrowly avoiding salmonella.

But let's fight these negative emotions. Let's just make the most of the light and fluffy chocolate roulade (sob) or dimple our buttocks with the coconut and pineapple terrine (a quick howling to the moon). Let's not think of how it usually is, let's just enjoy how it can be. Darling, we'll always have Chipping Campden.

CLENT

The Bell and Cross ★

Holy Cross, Clent, Worcs, DY9 9QZ.
01562 730319. Fax 01562 731733.

This listed white building nestling at the foot of the Clent Hills has one huge advantage in the world of pub grub – it is the business and home of top chef Roger Narbett, who runs this highly-successful venture with capable wife Jo.

The emphasis is on modern, satisfying fare that wouldn't be out of place in a swish little bistro - grilled Scottish rib-eye steak with frites, Cornish seafood fishcakes with prawns, bruschetta of tomato confit and English goat's cheese. Quality is evident throughout, from trusty risottos (often with wild mushrooms as the vegetarian choice) to farmhouse terrines.

It's confident, knowing stuff combining the most appealing of contemporary trends with a little top chef turbo-charging - a special of red bream was transformed by a wonderful mushroom velouté sauce while what may seem common-or-garden - marinated chicken for example - gets a transformation, here with the accompaniment of a Middle Eastern potato casserole.

The pubby look has been carefully preserved, with the various little rooms still intact, having escaped the late 20th century developers' hatchet job that ruined so many traditional inns. History is treasured here - one part used to be a butcher's shop and still has the old meat hooks in the ceiling. There is also a sizeable garden with plenty of tables for drinking and dining al fresco. Booking is always advisable.

British/European.

Mon-Thurs
12-2, 6.30-9,

Fri/Sat
12-2, 6.30-9.30.

Sun
12-2.30.

CC
(no Amex; slips closed).
Wheelchair access.
A/C.
Free range.
2+ V.

Starters
£3.50-£6.75.

Mains
£8.75-£13.95.

Desserts
£3.95-£4.50.

Sun L
£11.75 -2 courses,
£13.75 - 3 courses.

"A vegan going to a restaurant is a bit like someone going to a soccer match and demanding to see rugby." - I
Laurence McCoy, wine writer

Fountain Inn

Adams Hill, Clent, Worcs, DY9 9PU.
01562 883286. Fax 01562 886491.
Email richard@thefountaininn.freeserve.co.uk

Eclectic
Mon-Sat
12-2.30, 6-9.30.
Sun
12-8.
CC
(no Amex; slips
closed).
Free range/
organic.
2 V.
Starters
£2.95-£7.95.
Mains
£7.95-£15.95.
Desserts
£2.95-£4.25

Clent is rural enough and yet within easy reach of Birmingham for the Fountain to do more than averagely well out of visiting Brummies who fancy a night, or a lunch, in the country. The Clent Hills at weekends are alive with the sounds of 'Awlroight?'

The well-upholstered chef-patron of the Fountain, a Brummie himself, provides the sort of cabaret act as the loud, jokey mine host that his punters clearly love. Especially when it comes to 'cheeps! You can't have too many cheeps!'

The food is generally stocky pub grub, with some dishes more successful than others. The legend in its own lunch and dinner time is the lamb pot roast, an enormous great plateful of meat cooked long and slow till it almost falls off the bone. Certificates should be available for those who can finish it.

No frills then but a pleasant place with the right sort of pubby feel, even if it is mostly full of diners. It gets some good beers too.

CORSE LAWN

Corse Lawn House ★

Corse Lawn, Glos. GL19 4LZ.
01452 780771. Fax 01452 780840.
Email: hotel@corselawnhouse.u-net.com
Website: www.corselawnhousehotel.com

French-influenced
Modern British
Every day
12-2, 7-9.30.
CC
(slips closed).
Wheelchair access
(+WC).

A dream of a place situated out in gorgeous countryside near Tewkesbury, this exquisite, listed Queen Anne house has before it what you may think is a large and lovely duckpond. But the history of the place tells you it was once a drive-through coach wash (and inevitably, I suppose, horse wash)

It's just the sort of quirky little detail that might be expected in this top quality venture run by the Hine family of Cognac fame. Corporate, chain-style anonymous it ain't; there is real personality in evidence here, from the hearty, gruff, front-of-house style to the tantalising menu.

Food masterminded by Baba Hine in the kitchen supplies the bistro as well as the restaurant (there are also tables outside) and remarkable food it is too - confident and knowledgeable with bags of well-balanced flavours and an imaginative marriage of English and French.

The impressive kitchen skills have no airs and graces but an impeccable sense of taste. They may conjure up ballotine of duckling with spiced orange salad, smoked eel salad with pancetta and horseradish cream (both starters) or pigeon breasts with red wine, beetroot, barley and sausage or haunch of venison with crushed swede, chestnuts and red wine sauce. Big, rustic, comforting.

Desserts, in particular a memorable lemon tart with lemon ice cream, are excellent and the strong wine list (with a great range of Cognacs, as you'd expect) is a cause of some justifiable pride.

A perfect spot for a drive out on a sunny Sunday.

3 V.
Free range/
organic.

Starters
£3.95-£9.95.

Mains
£8.95-£27.50.

Desserts
£3.95-£5.95.

Set menus
D
3 courses £27.50.

L
3 courses £18.50,
2 courses £16.50.

Struggling for a wine to go with chocolate? One wine buff suggests Moscato d'Asti (a light, slightly fizzy, slightly sweet Italian) or a Madeira, while another wine fan swears by Chateauneuf du Pape.

DORRIDGE

Moat Manor Hotel

Four Ashes Road, Dorridge,
Solihull, B93 8QE.
01564 779988. Fax 01564 771331.

Traditional British
Mon-Sat
12-2.30, 7-10.30.

Sun
12-2.30.

CC
(no Diners; slips
closed).
Wheelchair access
(+WC).
1 V.

L
£18.95 – 3 courses,

D
£32.95 – 3 courses.

It may be difficult to track this place down (it's off the beaten track by a riding school) but the locals - who don't have too much fine dining choice locally apart from Nuthurst Grange - have clearly decided it's worth the effort.

It hasn't been in the new owners' hands all that long but they've already made their mark with use of colour - many of the hotel's rooms are luxuriously hued (take your sunglasses) and the building's yellow exterior is a bit of a shocker.

Things are more restful, colour-wise in the large, more traditional restaurant which offers good value set-price meals in a comfy environment. In the generous and ambitious menu, luxury ingredients pop up all over the place and the cooking, aiming at the classier end of modern thinking, is more than competent.

DORRINGTON

Country Friends ★

Dorrington, Shrewsbury SY5 7JD.
01743 718707.
Email: countryfriends@ukonline.co.uk

Modern British
Wed-Sat
12-2, 7-9.

CC
(no Amex. Diners;
slips left open).
Wheelchair access.
Organic/free
range/local.
1V.

L
£2.75-£10.

D
3 courses £29.90,
2 courses £27.50.

The main claim to fame of this half-timbered old place on the A49 is its leisurely Victorian breakfasts, which it offers at several points during the year. A wonderful thought in our time-starved world.

Otherwise, chef-patron Charles Whittaker, the bow-tied one, does a damned fine job with more regular restaurant hours - and with far better than regular restaurant fare.

The interior isn't, to be honest, hugely prepossessing - it's all a bit anaglypta and little prints among the beams - though the dining room is nicely formal, with fresh flowers and properly crisp cloths on the silver-crueted tables. Elegant touches include crimped pats of butter and gold-rimmed fine white china.

The best thing, as it should be, is the food, though the warm, homely service is much appreciated too. Following the seasons is a sensible priority; perhaps there'll be an asparagus sauce with halibut, a simple collection of great tastes all allowed to speak for themselves. A sweet potato purée and a piquant sauce make calf's liver a satisfying main course, as is braised guinea fowl with shallots and garlic. Nothing convoluted then, just first class food that makes you sigh happily at the end.

Puds, gratifyingly, keep to the same high standards. Chocolate tart with pistachio ice cream and a pear mousse trapped delightfully in a brandy snap sandwich both got top marks.

Petit fours and coffee are needed to complete the experience and both are very good. Rooms available for those too blissed-out to drive (although when the roads are quiet, the journey to Birmingham takes less than an hour).

ETTINGTON

Chequers bar and restaurant ★

91 Banbury Road, Ettington, nr Stratford-upon-Avon, Warks, CV37 7SR.
01789 740387. Fax 01789 748097.

Chequers has clearly decided its future lies in the direction of food rather than pints of ale. This is more a restaurant with beer than a pub with food; although a smallish bar gives a nod towards its local hostelry status.

Ettington isn't much more than one street. It may not have the chocolate-box charm of some of Warwickshire's more photogenic villages but it's still worth a visit because of the food here.

Some dishes sound decidedly grand - a jambonette of duck with a venison, bacon and red wine

Modern British

Tues-Thurs
12-2, 7-9.

Fri/Sat
12-2, 6.30-9.30.

Sun
12-3, 7-9.

CC
(no Amex, Diners).
3 V.

Starters
£2.75-£7.50.

Mains
£6.50-£16.

Desserts
£4.

Set L
£12 - 3 courses
(Tues-Sat).

stuffing on a compote of leeks with orange and cardamom dressing. And that's just a starter!

There's a lobster tank too for those who like to pick their victims personally but it's a little more down to earth elsewhere in the menu, though still high quality - perhaps chargrilled porterhouse steak, scallops, supreme of chicken or pork pavé. French influences pop up here and there, a Pernod and saffron sauce with sea bass or port, vanilla and thyme jus with slow-roast lamb all indicators of the kitchen's high ambition.

FAWSLEY

Fawsley Hall Hotel

Fawsley, near Daventry, Northants, NN11 3BA.
01327 892000. Fax 01327 892001.
Email: info@fawsleyhall.co.uk
Website: www.fawsleyhall.co.uk

Classic

Mon-Fri
7-9.30am,
12-2, 7-9.30.

Sat
7.30-10, 12-2,
7-9.30.

Sun
7.30-10,
12-2, 7-9.

CC
(slips closed).
Organic / free
range.
1 V.

Starters
£8-£13.50.

Mains
£17.50-£23.50.

Desserts
£8-£16.

Set L
£15 - 2 courses,
£19.95 - 3 courses.

Dinner
£31 - 3 courses.

Just over the border from Warwickshire and nicely close to Althorp for Princess Diana fans, Fawsley Hall is an impressive stately pile - more a hamlet than a house, with its wealth of buildings.

It was restored from a near-ruin in the 1970s and although the aim is high luxury, it can have a bit of a corporate feel about it (it is a popular conference centre).

The food aims to impress and prices are high. Expect an offal lot of à la carte grandeur with a salad of pig's trotter, sweetbreads, celeriac remoulade, quail's egg and balsamic jus or 'confit'd' guinea fowl and foie gras terrine with gewurztraminer jelly (both starters). Main courses can be equally fancy - a fillet of brill gets chicken and truffle mousse, crushed ratte potatoes, roast salsify and sauce lie du vin.

Not everything succeeds the way it should for the price. And talking of price - the wine mark-up is terribly steep. A service charge of 12.5 per cent is also added to bills.

GREAT WOLFORD

Fox and Hounds ★

Great Wolford, near Shipston-on-Stour,
Warks, CV36 5NQ.
01608 674220. Fax 01608 684871.

Another of those quintessential, honey-coloured Cotswold pubs, the Fox and Hounds is perfectly sited for tourists right on the Warwickshire/ Oxfordshire border.

You can tick the requisite items off the perfect country pub checklist - stone-flagged floors, a real fire in a great inglenook fireplace and proper beams.

The classy but comforting food reflects the interests of its new owner - food writer and specialist Wendy Veale. It's modern rustic and kept fairly simple but flavours are beautifully handled and truly appealing.

Soup may be carrot, honey and ginger, a confit of duck leg may be accompanied by orange and endive salad while salmon, cod and coriander fishcakes get a lime and caper mayonnaise. Mains are packed with taste, whether it's baked cod on Puy lentils with a crispy bacon and horseradish sauce, Cumberland sausage on champ or mushroom and gorgonzola tartlet with a salad of rocket, baby spinach, tomato and pine nuts.

Modern British.

Mon-Sat
12-2.30, 6-11.

Sun
12-3.

Wheelchair access.
3 V.
Local,
free range.

Starters
£3.25-£6.50.

Mains
£8.50-£13.95.

Desserts
£3.25-£4.50.

HAGLEY

West One

159 Worcester Road, West Hagley, Worcs,
DY9 0NW. 01562 885328. Fax 01562 887444.

Youthful and trendy, this little bar and bistro has been a big hit in the village whose main claim to fame is good schools and a lord married to a round-the-world yachting heroine up at the big house.

The chrome tables on the decking at the front get very full when the weather's fine - an oddly

Modern British

Mon-Fri
12-3, 6-10.

Sat/Sun
11-10.

CC
(slips closed).
Wheelchair (+WC).
A/C.
3V.

Starters
£3.50-£4.75.

Mains
£5.75-£9.95.

Desserts
£3.50-£4.25.

continental sight in this part of Worcestershire.

Inside, all is dark wood tables and blinds, nice bits of modern artwork and up-to-the-minute design.

Food keeps to a similar bracket - a fusion of Med, bit of Brit and touches of Thai. Very appealing too. Expect some striking touches among the good pasta, fresh fish, great chips and good puds. A nice range of beers and wines.

HAMBLETON

Hambleton Hall ★★

Hambleton, Oakham, Rutland, LE15 8TH.
01572 756991. Fax 01572 724721.
Website: www.hambletonhall.com

Modern British.

Every day
7.30-9.30am,
12-1.30, 7-9.30.

CC.
Organic.
Wheelchair
access.
10 V.

Starters
£9.50-£22.

Mains
£16.50-£32.

Desserts
£9.50-£20.

Set menu (Mon-Fri)
L
£16.50 - 2 courses,
£21 - 3 courses.

D.
£29.50 - 2 courses,
£35 - 3 courses.

I know that the east Midlands has been sadly neglected and I apologise. But this place simply demanded to be included - and what an absolute joy it was to visit.

Hambleton Hall has a Michelin star thanks to its ferociously busy TV chef Aaron Paterson (star of the Carlton Central series Wild About Food in which he does everything from diving for scallops to foraging for wild mushrooms).

His intense care for ingredients is more than matched by technical skill and mastery of presentation. Have asparagus here and it may well arrive in a perfect puff pastry box with the spears poking neatly out of the lid. Impeccably sourced meat and game will be impeccably sauced and garnished with the best of whatever the vegetable world can offer in season, with portions and flavours in utter harmony.

Game is a particular favourite, perhaps a tartlet of wood pigeon and wild mushrooms with Madeira sauce. This is the haute couture of the food world - braised tronçon of turbot with fondant potatoes or honey-roasted duck with orange and ginger sauce.

But better than the food - amazingly - is the venue. Here is a glorious country house in fine grounds which gazes out on to beautiful Rutland Water (now home to breeding ospreys). It feels like an island - and one which manages to offer utter luxury but with no pomp, the perfect combination for any top flight restaurant and hotel.

Expect every wish to be granted, every care soothed, every nagging worry consigned into the waste basket which is the real world. Of course it costs but nothing should be allowed to trouble the blissful Hambleton mode.

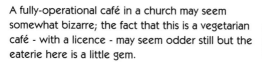

HEREFORD

Café @ All Saints

All Saints church, High Street, Hereford, HR4 9AA. 01432 370415. Fax 01432 344428. itsall@allsaintshfd.demon.co.uk

A fully-operational café in a church may seem somewhat bizarre; the fact that this is a vegetarian café - with a licence - may seem odder still but the eaterie here is a little gem.

Bill Sewell, who runs the vegetarian restaurant The Place Below in London, is the cook behind the menu although the café is completely owned by the church, which also receives all the profits.

Its Christian credentials are therefore beyond reproach but this is no hair shirt experience, as the licence may have led you to suspect. The look manages to be both modern and friendly and yet perfectly at home within the impressive aged church surroundings. One would imagine that pale wood contemporary bistro chairs, strip flooring and simple streamlined lines would jar but they sit underneath these austere arches very nicely indeed.

Forget booking, it's first come, first served and portions are of starving trencherman dimensions. If you feel your plate starting to drag as you take it along the motorway services-style serving hatch, don't worry - you're not suffering from some muscle-wasting disease, it's just the enormous amount of food that's weighing it down.

Vegetarian

Mon-Sat 8.30am-5.30.

Eve dinners quarterly.

CC (slips closed). Wheelchair access (+WC). Local/organic/ free range.

Starters £1.95.

Mains £4.60-£5.65.

Desserts £1.95.

Hearty comfort is the guiding principle. Soups are thick enough to stand your spoon in, there'll be quiches, loaded no doubt with rustic cheeses or maybe there'll be a Moroccan casserole with almond and currant bulghur. Local produce is well-used.

Because the presumption seems to be that you won't be eating again for a year or two, there'll also be salads and hunks of tasty bread (contemporary stuff too, like rosemary focaccia). Puddings as well, if you can cope.

The value is exceptional and the style cheery. They could feed the 5,000 but of course, they wouldn't use the fish.

Castle House Hotel ★

Castle Street, Hereford, HR1 2NW.
01432 356321. Fax 01432 365909.
Email: info@castlehse.co.uk. Website:
www.castlehse.co.uk

Innovative modern British with classical French undertones.

Every day 7-10am, 12-2, 7-10.

Children (up to age 8). CC (no Diners; slips left open). Wheelchair access (+WC). 1 V. Local/organic/ free range. A/C.

L £19.95,

D £29.95 (both 3 courses).

Not many new places, not even ones as swish as this, would normally hope to pick up four AA rosettes in their first year. But Castle House has managed not just that but has also scooped the title of AA hotel of the year.

This is elegance on a superb scale; fine dining as it should be. An experience of such pure hedonism, it must be the hotel equivalent of a heavenly massage.

Prices, considering the league they're in, are actually quite sensible - £29.95 for three courses. But beware the bumping up of the wine bill - the cheapest bottle here is £19 from a superb and enormous list that goes past the £200 mark.

But if you're celebrating, who cares? And this is just the sort of place to come if you are, especially if you're itching to get out a posh frock. Because it's a hotel, there are guests trooping in their casual gear as well but Castle House is really far too well-mannered to mind either way.

An elaborately French menu gives you four options at each course and lets you know precisely the sort of top-class gallic territory you're in. Local produce is abundant - Herefordshire beef, particularly, with an upwardly-mobile steak and kidney pudding in one instance - and artistry and hugely labour-intensive preparation are evident throughout. If you ever wondered just how good a 'compression' of carrot and gruyere could be, this is the restaurant you simply must visit.

The dining room is tranquil and in perfect understated taste, the service is faultless and the experience one to savour for a very long time.

Floodgates Brasserie ★

Left Bank village, Bridge Street, HR4 9DG.
01432 349009. Fax 01432 349012.
Email: dining@leftbank.co.uk
Website: www.leftbank.co.uk

Imaginative bistro fare

Mon-Sat 10-10.

Sun 10-9.

CC (no Diners; slips left open). Wheelchair access (+WC). Organic/free range/local. 2 V.

Starters £3.25-£4.95.

Mains £5.25-£12.95.

Desserts £3.50-£8.45.

Set menus for groups.

Floodgates is the relaxed sibling to the fine dining of La Rive and the Castle House hotel (see separate entries); all are owned by, and the brainchild of, Dr Albert Heijn, a fabulously wealthy Dutch guy whose own estate in Hereford provides the livestock which ends up on all the menus.

Floodgates and La Rive are part of the Left Bank village, a modern block right on the banks of the Wye which also houses decent food shops, a café and bar.

If the weather's fine, grab a table outside, whether it's just for a coffee or a chunky club sandwich or a hearty meal. The service is solicitous but relaxed, the decor colourfully modern and the food reliably good quality and imaginative.

Starters might include nice updates on brasserie classics, such as a haddock brandade, and there are plenty of little Dutch touches - spiced red cabbage with the confit duck leg or bitter ballen with zannse mustard.

Tempura of vegetables made a snackily-satisfying veggie main course, a big plateful of courgette, mangetout, carrot, cauli and peppers in crispy batter and drizzled with a jammy yet lively chilli sauce.

Seared loin of tuna on lemon and herb pappardelle pasta was well-cooked and delicious, with a fresh citrus sauce to punctuate the fish's natural oiliness.

Those with a sweet tooth should try the collection of mini desserts (for two), a delightfully satisfying range of gooey chocolate brownie, superb sherry trifle (I'm not usually a trifle fan but I loved this), blueberry parfait and raspberry and almond tart.

La Rive ★

Address as for Floodgates, above

The soothing and luxurious world of formal dining is made even more special when the restaurant has a great view and that, happily, is the case here. I'm not talking about the tailcoated French waiters, splendid though they are, but the sight of la rive itself, the Wye, grandly coasting by the restaurant complex.

It was a shame that the weather let us down and we weren't able to sit outside on the cruise deck-style balcony to make the most of it. But it was no great hardship to sit in the calm, pale cream interior and listen to the pianist play as the staff scurried about looking after our every whim.

The menu follows the same principles and style as Castle House, with four options at each course. The style is high French but using a great deal of first-class local produce and it's a marriage made in heaven, thanks to a lot of hard work in the kitchen.

This is grand, not simple, food - although the menu promises that if you want something simpler, then they'll make it for you. But dishes such as an exquisite salad of runner beans, pancetta and veal sweetbreads with a liquorice jus and apple glaze (a starter though it sounds like a main course) and delicious pot roast quail with chorizo and basil brandade and buttered cabbage - this is the sort of complexity that makes most diners want to eat out anyway, surely?

Vegetarians may find there is nothing on the menu but, naturellement, dishes will be made. Roast asparagus spears with morel cream and tiny nests

Anglo-French with a hint of fusion

Mon-Fri 12.30-2, 7-9.30.

Sat 7-9.30.

Sun 12.30-2.

CC (no Diners, slips left open). Wheelchair access (+WC). A/C. Local/free range/organic. 1V.

L £14 - 2 courses, £18.95 - 3 courses.

D £29.95 - 3 courses. Set menus available.

of spinach holding poached quail's eggs was a very good off-the-cuff offering.

Desserts balance indulgence and delicacy very capably; there's even a touch of whimsy. A parfait of white chocolate and Ristretto arrived with little brandy snap-like sesame wafers holding malt whisky and Coke ice. Very sophisticated but not stuffy - rather like La Rive itself.

HOCKLEY HEATH

Nuthurst Grange ★

Nuthurst Grange Lane, Hockley Heath, Warwickshire B94 5NL. 01564 783972. Fax: 01564 783919. Email: info@nuthurst-grange.com Wesite: www.nuthurst-grange.com

Modern British

Every day 7-9.30am, 12-2, 7-9.30.

CC (slips closed). Wheelchair access (+WC). 3 V.

Barely more than a slip road's length from the M40 is this fine country house hotel, all elegant grounds, squashy sofas by roaring fires and big curtains.

Its restaurant is formal with an ambience of almost unconcerned luxury. Behind the ease, however, is a lot of graft, with the hard-working kitchen offering homemade breads and petit fours as well as the choice available in two set menus.

L Starters £6.50-£8.50. Mains £12.50-£17.50. Desserts £5.50-£7.50. Or £12.95 - 2 courses, £16.95 - 3 courses.

D - menu 1: £29.50 - 3 courses;

menu 2 - £35 - 2 courses, £45 - 3 courses. Wine menu - £35 - 4 courses with wine.

Naturally, the bill is on the steep side - two set menus offer three courses and coffee for either £29.50 or £45. A four-course menu including wines is £35.

ILMINGTON

Howard Arms ★

Lower Green, Ilmington, near Shipston-on-Stour, Warks, CV36 4LT. 01608 682226. Email: howard.arms@virgin.net Website: www.howardarms.com

Modern British

Mon-Thurs 12-2, 7-9.

You don't have to be a tourist to admire the Cotswold perfection of this glorious stone-built place gazing over a little village green but it probably helps.

Fri/Sat
12-2, 7-9.30.

Sun
12-2, 7-9.

CC
(no Diners, Amex;
slips left open).
Wheelchair access.
A/C.
Organic/free
range/local.
1 V.

Starters
£3.50-£6.

Mains
£8.50-£13.

Desserts
£3.50-£4.50.

Grab a comfy chair and find a table (if you can) in the bar or snug or dining room of this civilised, award-winning free house and enjoy some fine ales (including Everards' Tiger and Marston's Pedigree) along with some home-made treats by the real fire.

There's also a more-than-decent wine list to accompany a thoroughly indulgent menu that proudly makes the most of its hostelry heritage. Beef, ale and mustard pie, chargrilled Barnsley chop, a trio of Warwickshire 'wizzer' sausages and roast cod with pea purée may provide the ballast while the hearty approach also makes itself felt through gentler fare - local asparagus is dished up by the half-pound (with hollandaise sauce), while chicken supreme is stuffed with crumbed ham and gruyere.

Mediterranean flavours are used in an almost iconoclastic way. Houmous, olive oil and mint accompany that Barnsley chop (Yorkshiremen may need to lie down in a darkened room) and a pork tenderloin is pancetta-wrapped and served with roasted courgettes.

An ample pudding list continues the to-hell-with-the-diet factor. Ginger syllabub, Mrs G's toffee meringue and some excellent artisan cheeses (try the Berkswell or wonderful Yorkshire Blue, one of my favourites) are just a few of the possible temptations crying out to be enjoyed.

Three rooms available too.

KENILWORTH

Simpsons ★★

Classical with
modern
French/British
touches.

Mon-Fri
12.30-2, 7-10.

Sat
7-10.

101/103 Warwick Road, Kenilworth, Warks, CV8 1HL. 01926 864567. Fax 01926 864510. Email: info@simpsons-restaurant.co.uk Website: www.simpsons-restaurant.co.uk

Don't even think about turning up at Simpsons in anything less than a trophy motor. That D-reg Metro will have you hanging your head in shame and parking round the corner when you see the swanky boys' toys lined up here.

Simpsons itself is a bit of a smooth motor - nothing so staid as a Roller but maybe a Porsche or top-range Audi. Classy, sleek and with a service completely slick but still human, this is one of my favourite places.

Even if you don't care about the softly-muted interior, the elegant suede seating or the mirrored walls, you must at least get enthusiastic about the food. It's fantastic and has won the place a Michelin star.

Chef-patron Andreas Antona (who early in his working life brought fame to the Plough and Harrow on the Hagley Road) has an assured, easy touch. But the kitchen is expert at maximising flavour and putting together masterful combinations rooted in classic French basics. Some dishes can look deceptively simple but mask a serious amount of highly-skilled work.

Seared scallops, black pudding, mushy peas, garlic and parsley cream, for example, hits so many different bull's-eyes - comfort, richness, freshness - that scallop fans may find themselves blubbering wrecks of gratitude. Red mullet with potato scales, fennel and artichoke barigoule is a work of art as well as a superb main course. There's a fixed price menu as well which is also excellent if (and quite understandably) not exactly bargain basement. Desserts are manageable too thanks to reasonable portion control.

CC
(slips left open).
A/C.
Organic/free range.
3 V.

Starters
£8.25-£12.50.

Mains
£17.50-£21.

Desserts
£6.50-£7.50

Set menu
£25.95 - 2 courses,
£33.95 - 3 courses.

Restaurant Bosquet ★

97a Warwick Road, Kenilworth,
Warks, CV8 1HP.
01926 852463.

Behind its English suburban home frontage, Restaurant Bosquet is a hive of Frenchness. Perhaps it's all the fervour of an ex-pat that makes chef-patron Bernard Lignier run his business on such resoundingly gallic lines.

The wine list is all French and the cooking is also French, although much if it is rustic in origin, cuisine de terroir rather than the cuisine of Michelin-starred grandeur - and as hugely flavoursome as that should imply. This big-flavoured

French

Tues-Sat
7-9.15.

CC
(no Diners;
slips left open).
V on request.
Wheelchair access.
Free range/
organic.

Tues-Fri
£26 - 3 courses.

Sat -
Starters
£8.50,

Mains
£17,

Desserts
£4.50-£6.

stuff takes no prisoners. Hefty cuts of meat are accompanied by hefty sauces, there's likely to be nothing on the menu for vegetarians (although there will be dishes made to order) and the menu doesn't change a lot. But the richness of tastes makes it a firm favourite with many, not least my partner who positively salivates at the thought of a visit to this, one of his favourite places.

The restaurant is very clearly also a home, looking if anything so much like a house rather than a restaurant, you feel you should ring the bell before entering.

Inside is a comfortable dining room, rooted decor-wise in the 80s, with a small bar at one end. A friendly front-of-house team is led by the owner's smiling English wife Jane who clearly knows the job backwards.

KNIGHTWICK

The Talbot

Knightwick, Worcs, WR6 5PH.
01886 821235. Fax 01886 821060.
Email: admin@the-talbot.co.uk
Website: www.the-talbot.co.uk

Eclectic
Mon-Sat
12-2, 6.30-9.30.

Sun
12-2, 7-9.

CC (slips closed),
Local/free
range/organic.
Wheelchair access.
1 V.

Starters
£3.50-£5.

Mains
£7-12.95.

Desserts
£3.50-4.

Set menus
available.

Try a half of This, That or T'Other in this friendly, family-run pub - for these are the specialist beers created by Philip Clift who runs the Teme Valley Brewery at the back of the pub while sisters Wiz and Anne deal with the hostelry side.

A family venture then, and a very popular one in this, one of the prettiest corners of Worcestershire, next door to Bromyard and by the snaking waters of the Teme. There's a simply-lawned garden but unfortunately the river is out of sight, though so close to hand.

There are two substantial dining areas as well as a terrace and bar. Food, quite clearly, is big business and the pub lays satisfyingly large store by local produce and quality sourcing. Dishes, which veer from typical pub grub, may feature polenta with wild mushrooms or crab and lobster with blinis. Various foodie trends are covered while a bar menu covers the simpler end. Service can be forgetful but it does get very busy.

LAPWORTH

The Boot Inn ★

Old Warwick Road, Lapworth,
Warks, B94 6JU.
01564 782464. Fax 01564 784989.
Website: www.thebootatlapworth.com

Mediterranean/
Pacific Rim.

Mon-Sat
12-2.30, 7-10.

Sun
12-3, 7-9.

CC (no Diners;
slips left open).
Wheelchair access.
A/C.
Organic/free
range.
4 V.

Starters
£2.95-£5.95.

Mains
£8.50-£13.

Desserts
£4.50.

Set menus
for groups.

The Boot is one of a handful of wonderful gastro pubs owned by businessman Paul Salisbury (who also co-owns the highly-rated Metro Bar and Grill in Birmingham).

As with his other ventures, the look is spot-on, service is youthful, slick and friendly and the food is bang up to date and delicious.

This has long been a favourite local watering hole - a modest-looking roadside pub which has been well and truly Salisburyed. The old peacefully cohabits with the new - nicely rustic furniture, tastefully paint-effected, the exposed beams are pale and interesting rather than painted black and hung with horse brasses. Food also becomes part of the decor; the pretty bottles of oil and balsamic on the off-white tables are a case in point - decorative as well as functional. A careful designer eye is at work here.

It's as upwardly mobile and moneyed as the clientele. Up in the stylish attic dining room, you can tuck into contemporary brasserie fare - seared rare tuna carpaccio with wasabi and pickled ginger, perhaps, or a courgette, pesto and feta tart to begin. Main courses may include the fishcake/quality sausage standards as well as lively pasta dishes and more adventurous fare like bang bang chicken.

The wine list is interesting (the delicious Macon is recommended) and there's a tranquil garden to Boot.

LICHFIELD

Chandlers Brasserie

Corn Exchange, Conduit Street, Lichfield, Staffs, WS13 6JU.
01543 416688. Fax 01543 417887.
Website: www.chandlersrestaurant.co.uk

Modern British/
continental.
Mon-Fri
12-2, 6-10.

Sat
12-2.30, 6-10.

Sun
12-2.30, 6-9.

CC
(slips left open).
A/C.
6 V.

Starters
£3.50-£5.95.

Mains
£8.50-£13.50.

Desserts
£3.95.

Table d'hote
Mon-Sat L
£8.50 - 2 courses.

Mon-Fri D
£10.75 - 2 courses.
£13.50 - 3 courses.

Sun
£13.50 - 3courses.

Behind its elegantly brick-arched frontage, Chandlers offers even more attractive settings - you walk into a sizeable, wooden-floored bustling bar in the lobby from which a brass-railed staircase swings off to the left. And through this is an airy atrium of a dining room with a high, domed ceiling bearing a huge chandelier.

The circular dining room is tastefully decorated and if space runs out here, there is a gallery offering more seating above it.

Service can be disconcertingly matey but food is of a decent brasserie standard - some good chicken livers with field mushrooms and chorizo on toast and pan-fried scallops and monkfish with prosciutto and garlic butter, for instance. It is big-hitting fare that doesn't hold back on flavour and generally doesn't disappoint, although some dishes from the cheaper set menu are not of the same standard. The à la carte and prix fixe do, however, mean a lot of choice, with a blackboard of fish specials also on offer.

Lloyds No 1 café bar

1 Bird Street, Lichfield, WS13 6PW.
01543 258525

Modern British

Mon-Sat
10-10.

Sun
12-9.30.

CC
(slips left open).
Wheelchair access
(+WC).
A/C.
4 V.

Starters
£1.99-£3.75.

A chain which offers chain-type fare but of a reasonable standard and in a pleasant, cream-walled, pale wooded environment. The building, a clean-lined cream affair, is pretty imposing too.

Robust, no-nonsense menu pleasers could include nachos (a filling selection for two) to artery-furring tortillas lavished with soured cream and spicy salsa. Starters like these may leave you rather spoilt for tasty main courses of Thai green chicken curry (much enjoyed) or a host of pasta dishes. Quorn is used as a veggie alternative for some creations, making for a sizeable vegetarian choice.

Mains
£3.99-£5.50.

Desserts
£2-£3.

2 meals for £5.99 deal also available.

Olive Tree

34 Tamworth Street, Lichfield. WS13 6JJ.
01543 263363.

There's no holding back with the trendy looks at this Mediterranean café and restaurant. Bright pink walls and string-tied napkins look good with the scrubbed pine tables and chef-watchers will be happy to hear that they can see their meal being prepared in the open kitchen at the end of the room.

Chicken, fish and pasta are the mainstays. Decent starters may include field mushrooms with prosciutto, garlic and ham or interesting salads, perhaps mixed leaves, with ricotta cheese, baby figs and plum dressing.

Tuna steak kept nicely rare may come with coriander and lime to cut the oiliness while monkfish tail could get extra zip with a lemon, tarragon and white wine sauce. Side veg are rather plain and service can slow down after main courses but the puds are still worth waiting for.

Mediterranean

Thurs-Sat
12-1.30;

Mon-Sat
6-10.

CC
(no Diners; slips closed).
Wheelchair access.
Organic/free range. 5 V.

Starters
£2.95-£4.95.

Mains
£7.25-£13.75.

Desserts
£3.50.

L
£6 - 2 courses.

D (Mon-Fri)
£9.95 - 2 courses,
£11.95 - 3 courses.

LLANFAIR WATERDINE

The Waterdine ★★

Llanfair Waterdine, near Knighton,
Shropshire, LD7 1TU.
01547 528214. Fax 01547 529992.

I suspect Ken Adams hasn't altogether made his mind up whether this is a pub or a restaurant but to my mind, it's definitely a pub - although the food is simply outstanding and worthy of any Michelin-starred restaurant. (He has a Bib Gourmand, the award for good food at reasonable prices, which seems a little mealy-mouthed for what's on offer here). The term gastro-pub could have been invented for this place.

Modern British

Tues-Sat
12.30-2, 7-9.30.

Sun
12.30-2.

CC
(no Amex, Diners,
slips closed).
Wheelchair access.
Organic/free
range/local.
2/3 V
(request when
booking).

Starters
£3.50-£6.50.

Mains
£9.50-£15.

Desserts
£4.25.

Also
D £25 - 3 courses.

Sun L
£13.50 - 3 courses.

With wife Isabel, who runs a charming front of house, he moved here from the Oaks restaurant in Ludlow (now Hibiscus, see separate entry). It's a simply glorious spot on the banks of the Teme, although the river flows by almost unseen below the level of their pretty garden. Llanfair Waterdine is a little hamlet a 40 minute drive or so from their old haunt and this place, down a narrow road by the pretty church, must have the best view around - of a green, tree-dotted hill where buzzards soar.

A bar menu offers excellent, simpler fare but the fine dining restaurant food is just superb, with a laudable emphasis on quality produce. (Some of this comes from the riverside garden tended by Isabel). The words 'organic' and 'free range' are regularly seen on the menu. Breads are first class and all home made. The pricing is excellent - especially a bargain Sunday lunch.

The 16th century black and white longhouse has some interesting tales to tell - mainly that Mallory planned his fateful Everest expedition in the bar. It's good walking country too, with Offa's Dyke a hop and a skip away. Pretty rooms available.

LONG MARSTON

La Blainvillaise

Barn Antique Centre,
Station Road, Long Marston,
nr Stratford-upon-Avon. CV37 8RB.
01789 721555.
Email: bruno@lablainvillaise.fsnet.uk

Traditional French
Mon-Fri
10-5.

Thurs-Sat
10-5, 7-9.30.

CC. (no Amex,
Diners)
Wheelchair access.
6 V.

Starters
£4.80-£4.95.

Mains
£4.80-£8.75.

Desserts
£2.50-£5.50.

This is a surprising place to find a little bit of France - within a rather nice antique centre in the rural splendours (ie middle of nowhere) of Warwickshire, not far from Stratford.

But it's worth a trip and not just for somewhere homely to recover with a coffee (although it is the splendid Illy brand) after the rigours of shopping.

La Blainvillaise, whose main dining room is a plant-filled conservatory, is serieusement Français - a French-run creperie and saladerie where you may find yourself struggling to remember your school French to help out the waitresses.

The food is simple but good and at very sensible prices. Eight salads offer an interesting range from niçois to black pudding with poached egg or chicken liver with raspberry vinegar (all just under £5). Les galettes, the savoury pancakes, include l'Ecossaise (smoked salmon with asparagus), Paysanne (smoked ham, egg and gruyere) or la Perigourdine (guinea fowl, mushroom and garlic), all just under £7.

The other choice range is 'Le Barbecue' where you can get a zippily fresh but simple piece of fish or meat with an elegantly-dressed salad. More exotic items - lobster perhaps, or crab - may also be available. Alcoholic accompaniments include an all-French wine list and some simple Normandy ciders. Perfect. You can indulge a sweet tooth with lovely fruity or choccy crepes and bought-in ice creams.

The place is very rustic but then so is the food - and all the better for it.

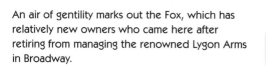

LOWER ODDINGTON

The Fox Inn

Lower Oddington, nr Stow-on-the-Wold, Glos, GL56 0UR.
01451 870555. Fax 01451 870669.
Email: info@foxinn.net
Website: www.foxinn.net

Modern British
Mon-Sat
12-2, 6.30-10.
Sun
12-2, 7-9.30.
CC
(no Amex, slips left open).
Wheelchair access.
Organic/free range.
2 V.
Starters
£3.95-£5.25.

An air of gentility marks out the Fox, which has relatively new owners who came here after retiring from managing the renowned Lygon Arms in Broadway.

This is typical, good Cotswold pub territory - ancient, creeper-covered stone without, real fires, beams and knick-knacks and a general sense of plumminess within. The decor is a gentle blend - it

Mains
£7.50-£10.75.

Desserts
£3.75.

has obviously been redecorated recently but with such care that the artistically-yellowed walls and sisal carpets hit no jarring notes in surroundings of such historical gravitas. (The fox theme here is not for the squeamish; hunt saboteurs could pick a better spot for their annual dinner.)

As for the food, the new pub standards are all here - mushroom risotto, fish pie, decent pasta et al - and they are all done robustly well and in quantities large enough to make even the ravenous tremble. A 'quad' of Cotswold sausages is a chunky starter. For those feeling more exotic, lamb tagine and couscous could hit the spot, or pesto-baked cod. Homemade and proud of it could be a motto; a dependable place with a decent wine list and a friendly welcome.

LOWER SLAUGHTER

Lower Slaughter Manor

Lower Slaughter, near Bourton-on-the-Water, Glos, GL54 2HP.
01451 820456. Fax 01451 822150.
Email: lowsmanor@aol.com
Website: www.lowerslaughter.co.uk

English/French

Sun-Fri
12.30-2, 7-9.30.

Sat
12.30-2, 7-9.45.

CC
(slips left open).
Organic/free
range/ local.
Request V on
booking.

L table d'hote
£12 - 2 courses,
£15 - 3 courses.

L alc
£40 - 3 courses.

D
£45 - 3 courses.

This magnificent country house is set in an impossibly-pretty village near Bourton-on-the-Water. Within a minute's drive is the equally-stunning Upper Slaughter with its Michelin-starred Lords of the Manor hotel.

Hence the problem - one will always live in the other's shadow and at the moment, the veil has fallen on Lower Slaughter. Lords of the Manor's recent Michelin-starred prominence has not helped.

The hotel itself is charmingly furnished and the restaurant is grand but not uncomfortable; light, airy and uncluttered.

The food is good, safe and classic. Lamb, asparagus when in season, great beef, perfect puds. The wine list is good, particularly the new world selection, the staff charming and attentive.

Ground-breaking is perhaps not the word to describe the place and/or its cuisine. But when a hotel offers comfort, attentive staff and well-cooked seasonal food, the word 'class' springs to mind. Lower Slaughter Manor is a leader in this field.

LUDLOW

The Courtyard

2 Quality Square, SY8 1AR.
01584 878080.

Ludlow, ah the blessed, most wonderful place, doesn't just have the Merchant Houses and the Mr Underhills, the Michelin-starred joints with the months-long queues to get in.

Oh no, it also has little gems like the Courtyard, a modest place with bare pine tables and a neat, housewifely interior that lives in the cobbled, delightfully-named Quality Square. The home-cooked fare emerging from the open-plan kitchen is interesting and pleasantly satisfying, whether it's a beef fillet with potato and celeriac rosti or honest-to-goodness broccoli and stilton quiche.

During one of my many visits to Ludlow, I asked a friendly owner of a B&B in the town where she ate - and this was the place. The Michelin-starred restaurants are much appreciated but seen by a lot of ordinary folk as for special occasions or visitors. Perfectly understandable. It's the everyday and yet decent quality places like this that keep the right balance for a gourmet capital.

As we went to press, the restaurant was only open at lunchtimes but this may change.

Modern British

Mon-Sat
12-2.

Wheelchair access
(+WC).
Local/organic/
free range.
3 V.

Starters
£2.75-£4.50.

Mains
£4.95-£6.95.

Desserts
£3.25.

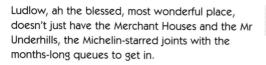

"La Galleria in Paradise Circus is a cracking place, the food's really smashing and it has a nice feel; it's a real family place. We go there for special occasions."
- Birmingham historian
Carl Chinn MBE

Hibiscus ★★

17 Corve Street, Ludlow, SY8 1DA.
01584 872325. Fax: 01584 874024.

Modern French

Wed-Sat
12.30-1.30.

Mon-Sat
7-10.

CC (no Amex,
Diners; slips
closed).
A/C.

L
£19.50 - 2 courses,
£25 - 3 courses.

D
£32.50 - 3 courses.

Menu degustation
£42.50.

The blessed Ludlow is also particularly lucky to host the first independent outing of the precociously-talented French chef Claude Bosi. He is an outstanding cook in this area, even with the amazing competition.

After winning a Michelin star for his previous employers at Overton Grange (just outside the town), the young French guy then set up shop with fiancée Claire (who used to waitress for Shaun Hill at the Merchant House, see below) in this charmingly oak-panelled, atmospheric spot right in the town centre.

The restaurant was once named Oaks, and run by Ken Adams (see entry for the Waterdine, Llanfair Waterdine). He was denied a Michelin star but Claude has already won one and is ambitious for more.

In my reckoning, he could easily win two; Shaun Hill thinks he may yet be worthy of three and could be right.

The couple have brought an easy, stylishly modern look into these olde worlde surroundings. Claude's cooking too has an exquisite lightness and artistry which, while it seems at home, still surprises. This is food which manages extraordinary depths and complexities of flavour and yet is almost ethereal.

So although you may think you can't manage the requisite four courses, you may surprise yourself (especially as there will be amuse-geules, appetisers and pre-desserts to contend with as well). Vegetarians are not the most important of people here; something will be available but it's best to mention it when booking.

Excellent ingredients matter, naturally, but there is an awful lot of work going on to make the already good into the sublime. Breads are all home-made, as are ice creams and sorbets, which are something of a house speciality. Expect some unusual flavours but also expect them to work.

I don't think you'll be disappointed - and the prices are less than grand country house hotels while offering far more.

The Merchant House ★★

Lower Corve Street, Ludlow SY8 1DU.
01584 875438.
Email: shaunhill@merchanthouse.org

Modern British
Tues-Sat
from 7pm.
Fri/Sat
L from 12.30.

CC
(no Amex, Diners;
slips closed).
Wheelchair access.
Organic/free
range.
2V if given notice.

Three courses
- £31.

Just a stroll from Ludlow's delightful town centre is the gourmet mecca known as the Merchant House. The home and business of top chef Shaun Hill, this is the restaurant that kick started the town's reputation as foodie capital of the shires (it is one of three Michelin-starred venues within roughly a square mile).

With all that kudos, you may be expecting something country house lavish, sumptuously comfortable and fearsomely expensive but it is none of these. The Merchant House is small and quite plainly furnished - it seems more money has been spent on modern works of art for the walls than the hard chairs for the diners.

It's a small restaurant (just 24 seats) and a one-man, two-woman show (his wife Anja and helper run front-of-house). Everything is kept simple and unostentatious, with bare tables and spare decoration.

Three courses now cost £31, a bargain for food from one of the top chefs in the country. The dishes here are always a surprise - appearing so artlessly simple and yet technically very accomplished. Freshness is all, from superb fish to great vegetables, and the cooking highlights rather than masks the natural flavours involved.

Signature dishes include monkfish with mustard and cucumber sauce but bourride (a rich fishy stew of turbot, sea bass and prawns) and risottos should also be mentioned in despatches. Desserts, like the rest of the menu, are reliably excellent.

Shaun Hill is a one-off. He doesn't go in for the fancy, cheffy stuff. Saddle of venison and goat's cheese gnocchi or rack of lamb with haricots, bacon and red wine sauce (two possible main courses) are just what they say they are. And you can bet they'll be superb.

Vegetarians who give advance warning will get their own menu but otherwise must take pot luck on the night.

Mr Underhill's ★★

P

Modern British.

Wed-Mon
7.30-8.30.

Free range/
organic/local.
V by request.
CC
(no Amex, Diners;
slips left open).

Three courses
£27.50.

Dinham Weir, Ludlow SY8 1EH.
01584 874431.
Website: www.mr-underhills.co.uk

One of my favourite restaurants, Michelin-starred Mr Underhill's beautiful riverside setting and sublime food have made it a top destination and not, happily, just for me and my equally overfed partner.

After several visits though, I still haven't seen the promised otters, kingfishers or badgers the area is allegedly home to and I'm now starting to wonder if those who claim to have seen them haven't been paying too much attention to Judy Bradley's excellent wine list.

The friendly 'restaurant with rooms' sits splendidly below Ludlow Castle and famously offers a single-option menu (with a set price of £27.50) for three courses with a choice at dessert.

Those who fear the lack of choice is a dreadful restriction should try it first (some poor indecisive souls actually find it a blessed relief). Chris Bradley's cooking is simply first-class and although his dishes may seem uncomplicated, it's amazing how he intensifies flavours, even in the most apparently simple dishes which at first glance night not seem all that interesting.

Great Witley asparagus (he's such a name-dropper) on a pancake of broad bean risotto with a champagne and chive beurre blanc is typically well thought-out but whether it tops his 'flavours of Provence' gateau or intense gazpacho

"A cucumber should be well sliced, and dressed with pepper and vinegar, and then thrown out, as good for nothing." - Dr Johnson

remains to be seen. Meat, fish or chargrilled veg acquire more flavour than they have any right to expect and puddings are equally heaven-sent. The wine list, though not cheap by any means, is a fascinating and impressively knowledgeable selection.

MALVERN WELLS

Cottage in the Wood ★

Holywell Road, Malvern Wells, WR14 4LG.
01684 575859. Fax 01684 560662.
Email: reception@cottageinthewood.co.uk
Website: www.cottageinthewood.co.uk

It's the stunning view here which has hungry diners regularly making the trek to Malvern. From this cosy hotel tucked high up on the hillside where Elgar loved to walk (you'll need to negotiate a hairpin bend or two), an immense vista lies out before you, a glorious vision of rural England at its most beautiful. It looks magnificent by day and magical by night.

Sensibly, the hotel's dining room windows are large enough to let you make the most of the scenery but the best place to eat at lunchtime, if the weather's fit, is outside in the pretty little garden. Tables here are at a bit of a premium, so it may be best to ask for one when you book. A superbly romantic spot.

It's a family-run and comfortable hotel, very eager to please. The bar area is full of squashy sofas and chairs - and you'll need to make sure you're sitting comfortably when you get the wine list. This is an enormous tome, a work of devotion. The choice is huge but the mark-up eminently sensible - not a combination seen very often. People can smoke here and they do - the dining room is non-smoking.

The food sets itself high standards and pretty well lives up to them. Satisfying stuff, basically, using well-proven flavour combinations. The French influence is strong; poussin may get a seasoning of thyme, garlic and bacon, while lamb's sweetbreads could arrive on linguine with a wild mushroom

Modern English

Every day
12.30-2, 7-9.

CC
(no Diners;
slips closed).
2 V.
A/C.
Local produce.

Starters
£4.25-£7.75.

Mains
£15.25-£18.50.

Desserts
£5.95.

Table d'hote

Mon-Sat L
£11.95 - 2 courses,
£14.95 - 3 courses.

Sun
£16.95 - 3 courses.

croustade. There are some surprising tastes too - a sultana and jasmine tea sauce with duck breast (also accompanied by Puy lentils and a confit leg).

You're unlikely to be disappointed and if you want to give that wine list a thorough testing, you can always stay the night.

Croque-en-bouche ★★

221 Wells Road, Malvern Wells, WR14 4HF.
01684 565612. Fax 0870 7066282.
Email: mail@croque-en-bouche.co.uk
Website: www.croque-en-bouche.co.uk

European with oriental influence

Thurs/Fri/Sat D from 7pm.

V by arrangemt. Organic/free range/local.

Thurs £27 – 3 courses, £30 – 4, £33 – 5 courses.

Fri/Sat £34 – 3 courses, £37 – 4, £40 – 5 courses.

Take no heed of apocryphal stories of an ogre ready to pounce on latecomers. While Robin Jones's manner may seem a little pernickety to some, Croque-en-Bouche has built an enviable reputation thanks to a genuine knowledge and passion for food and wine.

There aren't too many restaurants for instance where you are likely to be given the name of the fisherman who caught your turbot!

Punctuality is crucial because this is a two-person operation - Marion Jones takes care of the cooking and husband Robin does the rest at their elegant Victorian former bakery. But at least it gets you a useful half an hour to mull over the wine list, a fantastic range with a very reasonable mark-up.

With room for just 22, eating here is like being part of an extended dinner party. Meals are organised around three courses, with optional salad, cheese and puddings to follow and is good value.

This is foodie heaven, all bright, vibrant flavours with excellent, perfectly-matched ingredients, carefully sourced. Highlights from a wonderful inspection meal included a sensationally light and delicate filo croustade of Newlyn crab and lobster with pickled lemon and lemon and lime basils and a deliciously flaky Cornish turbot on minted couscous and broad beans with a grain mustard beurre blanc.

Then again, the rare fillet of Orkney beef, smoked by the restaurant, grilled and served with grilled peppers and aubergines shouldn't be left out, nor the meltingly soft Welsh Marches lamb marinated with parsley and olive oil and roasted with braised garlic and aubergine.

Cheeses, salads and puddings are all first class. Although the food may sound complicated, the overall impression is one of simplicity, with direct flavours shining through.

MORETON-IN-MARSH

The Marsh Goose ★

High Street, Moreton-in-Marsh,
Glos, GL56 0AX.
01608 653500. Fax 01608 653510.
Email: info@marshgoose.com

Superchef Sonya Kidney's confident, colourful cooking has a stylish home here in this ancient yet smart building in the centre of town. (She also has two pubs - the Churchill Arms at Paxford, see separate entry, and the Hare and Hounds at Foss Cross.)

The front of the slick operation is a café for daytime snacking and tea-drinking while the restaurant takes over the back, with smallish, cosy rooms, properly laid out for comfortable dining and enlivened with interesting little arty objets.

Service is smooth and can feel almost over-confident but the food, it has to be admitted, justifies it - the dishes are spectacularly flavoursome. Everything here is guaranteed to please - whether it's starters like salt cod fishcake with avocado and scrambled egg or monkfish with spiced chickpeas and Parma ham.

The emphasis is very much on intensely-flavoured meat, game and fish, which get equally sporty sauces and garnishes. There are capers and sweet

Modern British

Tues
7.30-9.15.

Wed-Sat
12.30-2.15,
7.30-9.15

Sun
12.30-2.15,

V on request.
CC
(slips left open).
Wheelchair access
(+WC).
Local/free
range/organic.

Starters
£7.95-£10.

Mains
£10-16.50.

Desserts
£6.50.

Set L menu

potato with a pavé of lamb, while duck breast gets the works with barley, artichoke, ginger, lime and sultana. It all sparkles with invention but vegetarians may well feel a bit left out. Something will be made for them but they may feel a bit of a nuisance.

OLDBURY

Jonathans Hotel and Restaurant

16 Wolverhampton Road, Oldbury, West Midlands, B68 0LH.
0121 429 3757. Fax 0121 434 3107.
Website: www.jonathans.co.uk

Classical British
Mon-Fri
12-3, 6-10.
Sat
6-10.30.
Sun
12-3.
CC
(slips left open).
Wheelchair access.
A/C.
2 V.
Local produce.
Starters
£4.90-£8.50.
Mains
£12.95-£18.50.
Desserts
£4.90-£7.50.
Set D menu
£28.95 - 5 courses.
Sun L
£15.90 - 3 courses.

Jonathans has spread over the years into a veritable warren of dining areas and chintzy hotel bits.

The Victorian restaurant is something of a local institution with its intensely-laden decor and chi-chi bits and pieces. The feel is added to by faux olde shopfronts elsewhere in the building, which provide useful advertising outlets.

It's all hugely camp but the menu's aspirations are serious enough to give the plastic a good run for its money. 'First removes' may include 'cornucopia of fish' or 'King Constantine's salad'. 'Main removes' are equally grandiose with 'Mrs Beeton's beef fillet', 'enveloped trout' and 'Worcestershire skillet'. A vegetarian main course of rarebit-stuffed mushrooms costs £12.95.

The greenery-laden Secret Garden (a conservatory-style room at the back of the building - though that may be letting the cat out of the bag) provides more relaxed dining, still with touches of Victorian whimsy ('Master Brown's parcel' is one main course).

OMBERSLEY

Crown and Sandys Arms ★

Main Road, Ombersley,
nr Worcester, WR9 0EW.
01905 620252. Fax 01905 620769.

Richard Everton of the village deli took over this rather odd-looking pub (the name is pronounced Crown and Sands) a while back and transformed it from a basically OK place to an extremely good one.

With its black-trimmed, curly-wurly roof lines, rather like exotic battlements, the mainly white hostelry has almost the look of a grand old cinema about it. It's large too and its interior has now been recreated in the form of three separate dining areas, all carefully decorated.

The bar section is the most pubbily casual but trendily interesting with it. There's lots of wood around and sparky little touches to update it here and there (dinky cacti, for instance). The other rooms are slightly grander and more restaurant, with murals and stylish furniture.

Dishes display cherry-picking from various cuisines, whether it's Thai flavours in a sauce for prawns, Indian spices like turmeric popping up in a rich veggie casserole based on flageolet, kidney and butter beans, or Italian creations with ciabatta, sun-dried tomatoes and mozzarella.

Crowd-pleasing stuff and, quite rightly, the crowds love it. A village as pretty as this is worth the ride anyway and the good wine list and some excellent beers add to the pleasure ratio. For the weekend indolent, there's also a fine brunch with the papers and endless coffee on Sundays.

Universal modern
Mon-Fri
12-2.30, 6-10.
Sat/Sun
12-2.30, 6-9.30.

2 V.
CC
(slips left open).
Wheelchair access
(+WC)
Starters
£4.25-£6.50.
Mains
£8.95-£21.95.
Desserts
£4.95.
Set Sun lunch
£16.95 - 3 courses,
£13.95 - 2 courses.

"My long-term favourite is the Eaton Hotel on the Hagley Road for quality, quantity and atmosphere. Lately I have been introduced to the Bay Tree in Edgbaston. Both are places where I can and do spend many happy hours."
- Ed Doolan MBE, BBC Radio WM

Modern British

Tues-Sat
12-2; 7-9.45.

Sun
12-2.

A/C.
CC (no Amex,
Diners; slips
closed).
1 V.

3 courses (D)
£27.95.

L
3 courses £17.95,
2 courses £14.95.

Venture In ★

Main Road, Ombersley, WR9 0EW.
01905 620552.

Pretty Ombersley is jolly lucky to have two quality eateries like the Crown and Sandys and the Venture In within a few yards of each other.

The Venture's young chef-owner Toby Fletcher actually worked at the Crown and Sandys before moving up the road into business for himself at this pretty and ancient black and white restaurant.

And very successful he's been too (and more power to his elbow) after a few years of going it alone. The bijou place has been redecorated, with a smart, modern, checked carpet and furnishings in warm orange tones blending in well with the ancient beams, inglenook fireplace and old stone.

I love the cooking here - it can be a bit of a blow-out but it's jam-packed with flavour. Toby Fletcher excels at getting maximum taste out of every ingredient. It's superb value too, with dinner starters such as pressed guinea fowl terrine with French bean and potato salad or home-smoked fillet of duck with spiced apple chutney.

Main courses keep to the same marvellous standard, whether an unctuous pot roast shoulder of lamb or delicious risotto (often the vegetarian option). The desserts are so good that I even asked for a recipe for one of them (not something I've done before or since) - a chocolate marquise that beat the competition into a cocked hat. (I have made it myself and although it's good, it's a bit of a faff and it never seems to taste as wonderful).

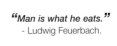

"Man is what he eats."
- Ludwig Feuerbach.

PAXFORD

Churchill Arms ★

Paxford, nr. Chipping Campden
Glos GL55 6XH.
01386 594000. Fax: 01386 594005.

Modern British

Every day
12-2, 7-9

CC
(no Amex, Diners;
slips left open)
Free range/
organic.
V on request.

Starters
£3-£7.

Mains
£7-£13.

Desserts
£4.

On a cosy little corner opposite the church in this tiny village, top chef Sonya Kidney's neat, unassuming stone pub looks rather unremarkable considering its fierce gastro reputation (she also has the Marsh Goose in Moreton-in-Marsh, see separate entry, and the Hare and Hounds at Foss Cross).

Inside, it's a bit on the cheek-by-jowl side but the look, with rustic wooden tables and chairs and a pretty, eclectic interior, is pleasant and informal - just the right sort of blend of trendy and tradition. And those cooking smells wafting in from the busy kitchen are simply fantastic, inspiring instant confidence.

The menu - chalked up on a blackboard on a central pillar of the pub - fires on all cylinders of a hot-wired foodie imagination. Some surprising combinations seem almost like wild gambles but inevitably, they really work.

As one of the most popular places around (now that the Stagg at Titley has got a Michelin star, how about this?), it gets very, very busy but they take care to make sure the drinking locals get looked after.

Vegetarians may well find nothing available on the list although the kitchen is more than capable of preparing something outstanding. They will do something for you when requested.

Rooms are available.

PEMBRIDGE

The Cider House restaurant

Dunkertons' Cider Mill, Luntley, Pembridge, nr. Leominster, Herefordshire, HR6 9ED. 01544 388161.

Seasonal/local/
imaginative.

Mon-Sat
10-5
(closed Jan, Feb)

CC
(no Amex;
slips closed).
Wheelchair access
(+WC).
Organic, free
range, local.
1 V.

Starters
£3.75-£5.50.

Mains
£9.75-£12.50.

Desserts
£3.50-£5.

If you're ever faced with a sunny day and wonder how to pass the hours then make the journey through this marvellous yet almost undiscovered county to Dunkertons.

It will feel pretty remote: Road names don't seem to exist out here and 'Luntley' is about as exact as the address gets but you'll get there (there are signs from Pembridge to help).

It's gloriously pretty; and not just as a precious piece of rural heritage. This 400-year-old building is also a fully-functioning cider mill where you can see the cherished old equipment and taste (and, hopefully, buy) all manner of its still and sparkling products.

But before all that, enjoy a meal in the restaurant which has a fantastic protected verandah with a wonderful view as well as lots of tables in the comfortably-rustic interior.

The food, prepared by a kitchen team led by Susie Dunkerton, has no pretensions. But it will, for the most part, be local and seasonal, honest and incredibly generous. If ever there was a ploughman looking for a good lunch, he should come here. The superb local cheeses are a particular high point and served in great hunks with homemade chutneys (also available to buy at the counter). Cider and perry, naturally, have starring roles.

A warm salad of broad beans and mushrooms has a light but tasty mint and garlic dressing, while spicy potted crab has strawberry salad and melba toast. Those are both starters (there's a choice of four). Mains may feature cider-braised leg of lamb with shallot, fennel and lemon potatoes or a courgette, pepper and almond crumble.

If you have any room left, try the superb organic ice creams. In fact, try them even if you think you haven't any room left. The brown bread flavour is just wonderful.

PERSHORE

The Epicurean ★

76 High Street, Pershore, Worcs, WR10 1DU.
01386 555576 Fax: 01386 555572.
Email: epicurean.restaurant@lineone.net

Modern global
Thurs, Fri
D only.
No CC.
A/C.
Free range/
organic.
V by arrangemt.
5 courses £32,
6 courses £37.

The opening hours for the Epicurean are so limited - just Thursday and Friday evenings - that you may suspect a bit of clever marketing is going on. But with chef-patron Pat McDonald busy with consultancy work (from the office upstairs) and TV (remember his troubleshooting chef role in C4's If You Can't Stand the Heat?), it's perhaps sensible.

But the best reason for going to the Epicurean, if I may say so in a shamelessly female shopper sort of way, is to ogle the furnishings. This place is so stylish it almost hurts. Where did they get those fantastic ice buckets? Those beautiful cruets? Look at the buckets of orchids! Can we get a catalogue?

The food, though interesting and in parts excellent, can't possibly impress to the same degree. Perhaps this is why we felt vaguely disappointed that we didn't enjoy it more, even though so much was good. Expectations had been raised sky high by the fact that behind the restaurant's small terraced frontage was a temple of good taste.

The ambitious set menu offers five or six courses of well-crafted and well-thought-out flavours with the emphasis on good ingredients. The first two courses may be a vine tomato soup with crab and basil crème fraiche, followed by some Italian cured meat with an asparagus dressing. Then there might be a salmon ravioli and a main course of roast coquelet with wild mushrooms before a lemon dessert and the cheese. They also offer a wine 'menu' with a different glass to accompany each course.

Mrs McDonald leads a solicitous service team. You will return home feeling not only full but vaguely troubled by a sense of furnishings inferiority.

PRESTON BAGOT

The Crabmill ★

Preston Bagot, Claverdon, Warks B95 5DR. 01926 843342. Fax: 01926 843989

Modern European

Mon-Fri
12-2.30, 6.30-9.30.

Sat
12-2, 6.30-9.30.

Sun
12.30-3.30.

CC
(no Diners;
slips left open).
Wheelchair access.
Free range.
3 V.

Starters
£4-£7.

Mains
£9-£16.

Desserts
£4-£5.

One of the best pubs around for food - and also one of the best-looking. Trendy is definitely the name of the game (like its siblings the Boot at Lapworth and Kings Head, Aston Cantlow) but there's no question of style over substance - the food is most certainly on a par with the decor and round here, that's a big compliment.

Flagstone floors, different coloured 'rooms' (just areas really) and bowls of fruit as objets d'art all set a very appealing scene and no doubt contribute to the pub's great success (its white roadside exterior wouldn't give you much of a hint as to how it looks inside).

Young, pretty, tightly T-shirted female staff may also have something to do with its allure, for one half of humanity at least. But this is far from bimboland; a smoothly-professional operation ensures good food and drink served efficiently and pleasantly.

And as for the food, it could be offered on prescription for those with a jaded palate. This is pub grub to blow the cobwebs away - youthful and vibrant, casual but chic, comforting yet zippily fresh.

There doesn't seem to be a duff thing on the Med-influenced menu, whether it's one of the heavenly pasta dishes, hearty meat fare or flavour-packed salads. The feel of quality is epitomised by excellent oils and sauces.

Prices are reasonable and booking is often necessary, especially at weekends.

PRIORS HARDWICK

Butcher's Arms

Church End, Priors Hardwick, Southam,
Warks, CV47 7SN.
01327 260504. Fax 01327 260502.
Email: enquiries@thebutchersarms.com
Website: www.thebutchersarms.com

A big menu and a big wine list (more than 200
choices) pile up the options at this hugely popular
14th century village pub.

The drive into rural Warwickshire will hopefully
build up a ravening hunger, for a hearty appetite
will be needed to appreciate the range of dishes
on offer. The list goes from the traditional to the
trendy but happily, they're as good with the simple
things as the more complex - a home-made
gravadlax can be just as satisfying as a grand main
of richly-sauced venison. Substantial puds should
see off any lingering hunger pangs.

Traditional British/
Portuguese/ French

Mon-Fri
12-2, 7-9.30.

Sat 7-9.30.

Sun 12-2.30.

CC.
Wheelchair access.
4 V.

Starters
£4.25-£13.

Mains
£12-£20.

Desserts
from £4.75.

Table d'hote
Mon-Fri L £16.50.

Sun £26.50.

SHATTERFORD

Dominiques

Bellmans Cross Inn, Bridgnorth Road,
Shatterford, near Bewdley, DY12 1RN.
01299 861322. Fax 01299 861047.

Dominiques is actually the restaurant side of a pub
and though it may be in deepest Worcestershire,
there's an overwhelmingly French influence going
on, thanks to the French landlord and chef - the
eponymous Dominique.

The long black and white building provides
ample space for both Dominiques (quite
traditionally formal with white-draped tables and
little copper pans for the veg) and the Bellman's
Cross bar (which has its own decent menu).
But it is definitely more an eating rather than
drinking establishment.

French-influenced
modern British

Sun-Fri
11-2.30, 6-9.45.

Sat
11-9.45.

3 V.
CC
(slips left open).
Wheelchair access
(+WC).

Starters
£3.50-£12.50.

Mains
£8.95-£15.95.

Desserts
£3.50-£4.50.

The food is substantial but also shows some nice touches of ambition. A terrine of foie gras gets a Cumberland sauce or there may be some home-smoking on offer - duck breast, perhaps, with some interesting berried accompaniments. Mains are strong on the big and meaty and have well turned-out garnishes, whether a fillet of beef Rossini with foie gras, toast and truffles on a madeira sauce or duck leg confit with prunes and cinnamon sauce on sweet potatoes. Fish gets the big taste treatment too with roast cod and mash or salmon supreme in filo pastry.

The wine list is a good one and offers non-French favourites, with some good choices from New Zealand and Alsace, as well as Italy, Australia, South America and South Africa.

SHIPSTON-ON-STOUR

Chavignol at the Old Mill ★

8 Mill Street, Shipston-on-Stour,
Warks, CV36 4AW.
01608 663888. Fax 01608 663188.
Email: chavignol@virginbiz.com

Modern European

Every day
12-2, 6.30-11.

CC
(slips left open).
Organic/free
range.
1 V.

3 a/c courses
- £40, L or D.

Also
table d'hote L
£18 - 2 courses,
£25 - 3 courses,

D
£30 - 3 courses.

Having gained plaudits and great critical acclaim in Chipping Norton, the Chavignol team have turned that eaterie into the brasserie Chav and made this new venture in Shipston their formal dining HQ.

And fine dining it certainly is, with the sort of ambition that determines to impress and the skill and artistry that consistently pulls it off. Don't expect anything here that doesn't take at least a couple of hours to create - starters may include a 'duo of hand-dived Scottish scallops roasted on haricot vert and red wine shallots, and marinated in honey and orange, with blinis' or maybe 'sautéed foie gras on mushy peas with rilette of Shipston duck and prune and cider compote'.

It's an extravagant menu but efficiently planned - the prix fixe lunch menu, for instance, includes adaptations from the à la carte, such as a main course pan-fried fillet of gilthead black bream with tapenade tagliatelle, Provençale veg and tomato vinaigrette - the same accompaniments that an alc starter of red mullet gets.

Despite the complicated ingredients and combinations, the dishes work well and are very understated and sophisticated. Presentation is also artistic - a starter of chicken liver parfait was a study in pastels with the parfait and accompanying plum mayonnaise arranged in neat ovoids around some salad with caramelised hazelnuts.

Service is formal and polished, the building is lovely, with terracotta floor tiles and pale cream walls, and the wine list is excellent. Prices are quite steep but when such huge efforts are made to turn a meal out into a special occasion, they do not seem unjustified. Five luxurious rooms, each designed after various regions of France, are available.

SHREWSBURY

Sol ★

82 Wyle Cop, Shrewsbury, Shropshire, SY1 1UT. 01743 340560. Fax 01743 340552.

Modern British

Tues-Sat
12.30-3, 7-9.

CC
(no Amex. Diners;
slips closed).
Wheelchair access.
1 V.

L - Starters
£3.75-£6.

Mains
£9-£15.

Desserts
£4.50.

D -
£28.50 - 3 courses.

Sol is a veritable temple to modern chic in the centre of venerable and sedate Shrewsbury.

The food is vibrant, rich and full of flavour - and is presented with as much style as the impressive surroundings. But the show should not detract from the essentials - here we have a sound grasp of the basics and only with these as a solid foundation does the lively, imaginative stuff pay off.

There are no unnecessary complications. Roast wood pigeon, for instance, gets a simple yet successful association with mustard leeks, baby beetroot and balsamic salad. It takes confidence to keep thing simple and Sol has earned its spurs. In fact, the only bad news is the long hike up several flights of stairs to the loos. 'You definitely need to be sober for this!' complained one reporter.

At busy times, service can slow down but Sol still more than repays a visit.

SOLIHULL

Beau Thai

761 Old Lode Lane, Solihull,
West Midlands B92 8JE.
0121 743 5355. Fax: 0121 688 5568.
Email: samson@beauthai.freeserve.co.uk
Website: www.beauthai.co.uk

Thai
Tues-Fri
12-1.30.
Mon-Sat
6.30-10.
CC
(slips left open).
Wheelchair access
(+WC).
A/C.
13 V + set menu.
Starters
£3.25-£6.25.
Mains
£3.45-£13.95.
Desserts
£2.50-£3.95.
Set menus
£14.95-£26.95.

There's no holding back with the decor at Beau Thai - murals of Thai fields and houses bring the walls glowingly to life, greenery spills out all over the place and a water feature adds a feng shui touch with the best sort of background sounds you can imagine. Restrained it ain't.

This is a faithful old standby of the Solihull restaurant scene and much-loved by an army of regulars. They're given an awful lot of choice to work through - pages and pages of dishes which may appear overwhelming to the uninitiated, although suggested set menus fill some of the space.

Duck, poultry, meat and fish abound in any number of variations which may include red or green curry, sauces such as satay and oyster, delicately cooked noodles and properly sticky rice. Coconut fried rice makes an interesting accompaniment and is perfect evidence of the sort of comforting flavours on offer.

For those worried about the heat, each dish is rated for spiciness by the number of chillies next to it. It may not have the magazine-style chic of the new Thai places in the city but it feels genuinely authentic and service from the traditionally-dressed staff is helpful and reassuringly friendly. Vegetarians are offered a great variety of dishes but the widespread use of fish sauce as a condiment can be a worry.

Rajnagar

256 Lyndon Road , Olton, Solihull, B92 7AW.
0121 742 8140/4842. Fax 0121 743 3147.
Email: info@rajnagar.com
Website: www.rajnagar.com

There are traditional-style Indian restaurants in every suburb across the land and the quality-driven Rajnagar is one of the thoroughly reliable. The decor is everything you'd expect of the genre and the food is quality, with lots of fish choice (a particular strength here - the monkfish massala is particularly worth trying).

With an undeniable feeling of pride, the service is still thoroughly friendly. Beer is probably the best accompaniment although the wine list offers east European and Aussie options.

All the old favourites are here but served fresh and with a feel for good spicing and quality. Sometimes it's the simplest things which reveal the most - and here, excellent, deliciously-spiced rice can tell you all you need to know about the standard of the kitchen.

Bangladeshi/
traditional Indian

Sun-Thurs
5-12.30.

Fri/Sat
5-1am.

CC
(slips left open).
Wheelchair access
(+WC).
A/C.
V set menu.

Starters
£2.95 average.

Mains
£8.75 average.

Desserts
£2.95 average.

Set menus
£16.95
(V - £12.95.)

STOURBRIDGE

French Connection

3 Coventry Street, Stourbridge,
West Midlands, DY8 1EP. 01384 390940.

Down one of busy little Stourbridge's side streets is this humble little bistro with deli attached. Both are worth a visit.

French Connection has obviously been modelled on a French café and it works, with its little, red, gingham-topped tables, red-striped walls and ceiling fans. A bit cramped (and nearly always busy with hungry shoppers) but it has a good feel and an authentic whiff of garlic.

Alongside the à la carte is a bargain, fixed-price lunch menu. Both list rustic but appealing dishes: A potage du jour comes in a tureen, there are country-style patés (including some good

Modern/traditional
French with some
European.

Tues-Sat 9.30-4.30.

Wed-Sat 6.30-10.

CC (no Diners;
slips left open).
A/C.
Free range/organic.
3 V.

Starters
£3.30-£6.95.

Mains
£5.95-£12.95.

Desserts
£2.95-£4.25.

Set L menu
7.95 or £8.95.

D
£15-£26.

vegetarian versions), hearty and good quality salads, and decent pasta, meat and poultry dishes. Fish also makes a regular appearance, whether roasted cod with cheese and herb crust or salmon in a creamy dill and saffron sauce. Mussels are a perennial favourite and dished up in a generous, fragrant bowlful rich with garlic and white wine sauce (and you get a bib too to protect your clothes). The dinner menu goes upmarket with dishes like sea bass or coq au vin.

Pizza Express

74 High Street. 01384 379358.
See Birmingham entry

STOURTON

The Fox Inn

Bridgnorth Road, Stourton, nr Stourbridge, West Midlands, DY7 5BL.
01384 87771.

Modern British.
Every day
12-2.30, 7-10.
CC
(slips left open).
Wheelchair access
(+WC).
A/C.
3 V.
Starters
£3.50-£5.
Mains
£6-£13.
Desserts
£3.95-£4.95.

A smart white pub in a particularly pretty corner of the countryside, the Fox has numerous attributes, not least its huge garden and smart little bistro.

There's a little conservatory too next door to the bar which can suffer from smoke drift (and the bar does gets its regulars - this is most definitely a pub with food attached).

There's a mass of food on offer with a big blackboard list of dishes in the bar and another menu for the bistro (though you can probably mix and match - we did for vegetarian fare at least).

The bistro is the smarter area to dine in, with its woody tones and blue and terracotta colouring. There are serious culinary efforts being made, with a mix and match of British, anglicised Med and Thai brasserie offerings.

STOW-ON-THE-WOLD

Hamiltons Brasserie

Park Street, Stow-on-the-Wold,
Glos, GL54 1AQ.
01451 831700. Fax 01451 831388.

Hamiltons looks rather like a little bit of Habitat suddenly descended on Agatha Christie territory but somehow, it all seems to work.

Stow is a glorious Cotswold town with plenty of tea shops, antique shops and traditional pubs - and of course, what it really needed was a bang up-to-date brasserie with streamlined pale wood, bare stone walls, zingy modern fusion cuisine and cutting-edge stylish china and cutlery.

And that's what it's got. A lively youthful imagination here takes expected centre-stagers and puts the unexpected alongside them. The ubiquitous roasted Mediterranean vegetables, for instance, find new life with artichoke pesto and toasted basil bread. Fishcakes (of salmon, smoked trout and dill) get fennel and almond salad. There's a bisque dressing for baked sea bass and basil noodles and a mango and sweet potato salsa for chicken breast.

Food is also art, with stylish creations placed carefully on huge white plates. This sort of thing doesn't come off if the flavours don't live up to the presentation but here, happily, it all works pretty well.

Fine, friendly service and a good wine list all add to the sense of bonhomie. And appealing desserts - perhaps a minted chocolate Gascony mousse or a blood orange brulée - certainly help that feeling of well-being. The perfect place, in fact, for a meal during those cheese awards in September when the town is busier with visitors than ever. Just be sure to book ahead.

Modern British with Mediterranean and Asian influences.

Mon-Sat
9-2.30, 6-9.30.

Sun
10-3.

CC
(slips left open).
Wheelchair access
(+WC).
A/C.
Local/free range.
3 V.

Starters
£3.50-£5.75.

Mains
£5.50-£14.

Desserts
£4.25-£4.95.

Smirking sous chef -
"I"m leaving to start on my own up the road. Thanks for teaching me everything I know."

Master chef – "That's OK (smile). I might have taught you everything you know but I didn't teach you everything I know!"

STRATFORD-UPON-AVON

See also Alderminster - Ettington Park;
Alveston - No 1 Pimlicos;
Armscote - Fox and Goose;
King's Head - Aston Cantlow
and Long Marston - La Blainvillaise.

Coconut Lagoon

21 Sheep Street,
Stratford-upon-Avon, CV37 6EF.
01789 293546. Fax 01789 297981.
Website: www.coconutlagoon.com

Southern Indian
Every day
12-3, 5-11.

CC.
Wheelchair access.
5 V.

Starters
£3.50-£11.50.

Mains
£7-£13.50.

Desserts
£3.25-£4.25.

Set menus
£21.75.

Vivid saffron, such a key spice in Indian cuisine, is also the colour of the walls of this recent arrival on the Stratford restaurant scene. With its contemporary style and rattan furniture, the look is modern-day colonial and very stylish and welcoming. The smart cocktails on offer fit the mood very well.

Decor apart, Coconut Lagoon also aims to differ from run-of-the -mill Indian restaurants by offering cuisine from the southern states.

Worth sampling from the starters is paneer roti, soft and tasty with the cheese fried with onions and tomatoes or highly-peppered Karaikudi minced lamb cutlets with almonds and sultanas. Fragrant main courses include a tasty fennel-flavoured lamb served with Indian salad or a delicious, baked stuffed pomfret. A class apart from the usual, with
prices to match.

*"Hope is a good breakfast,
but it is a bad supper."*
- Francis Bacon (who makes a good
breakfast, with eggs)

Desport's ★

13-14 Meer Street, CV37 6QB.
01789 269304.
Email: bookings@desports.co.uk
Website: www.desports.co.uk

Eclectic

Tues-Sat
12-2, 6-9.30.

CC
(slips left open).
Organic/free
range/local.
3 V.

Starters
£4.50-£6.50.

Mains
£11.95-£16.95.

Desserts
£5.50.

Set L
£5 - 2 courses,
£7.50 - 3 courses.

Set menus
available
or groups.

This sunnily-yellow first floor restaurant is girded by ancient beams befitting the building's aged origins and lit by some very smart, up-to-date wall lamps - it may be historic Stratford, in other words, but that's no reason why we can't be modern.

And modern it certainly is with a menu that instead of offering the usual starter, main course and pud sections splits the dishes into Earth, Land, Sea and Heaven (the last being desserts). Savoury dishes are offered in two sizes to give maximum choice. It's a neat idea that has served Paul and Julie Desport well since they set up shop here four years ago.

A background of working in top London hotels has left the couple with a resolutely quality approach to what they offer. It can't be an easy life producing everything from your own breads to the brandy snaps to serve with coffee but this virtue has its reward in the shape of a loyal fan base.

Presentation is thoroughly modern, as are the ingredients, with no fear of offal or exotic flavourings. Risottos are superb, soups comfortingly home-made, meat and fish expertly cooked with masses of fresh herbs, puds are a delight and the cheeseboard worthy of particular praise. Their set-price lunches are the best bargain around.

Veggie dishes generally are a strong point and amply illustrate Paul Desport's inventiveness in the kitchen. One of his winning risottos matched butternut squash with lentils and pumpkin seeds for a great, toasty combination.

Julie at front of house is friendly and efficient, serving up well-sized portions which make dessert a likely option rather than merely the preserve of the greedy.

The Opposition

13 Sheep Street, Stratford, Warks, CV37 6EF.
01789 269980. Fax 01789 299326.

Modern
English/French

Mon-Sat
12-2, 5-late.

Sun
12-2, 6-9.30.

CC
(no Amex, Diners;
slips left open).
Wheelchair access.
3 V.

Starters
£2-£6.95.

Mains
£8.50-£15.50.

Desserts
£4.50.

The Opposition may be an old stager on the
Stratford scene but its relaxed 'restaurant café'
approach is a popular one still for natives as well
as tourists.

Blackboards reel off a list of predominantly Med-
based favourites designed for mid-priced appeal.
Expect lots of fish - from decent salmon fish cakes
(perhaps with sorrel sauce and spinach), whole
lemon sole or trio of salmon; chunky meaty stuff -
whether steaks, chicken (in various national
versions); a reasonable vegetarian selection (a
goat's cheese salad perhaps or spinach and feta
pie) and golden chips.

Restaurant Margaux ★

6 Union Street, Stratford, Warks, CV37 6QT.
01789 269106.

Modern English
with a twist

Mon-Sat
12-2, 5.30-10.

CC
(no Amex;
slips left open).
Wheelchair access.
1 V.

Starters
£4.95-£6.

Mains
£8.50-£18.

Desserts
£4.95.

People don't just go to this trendy little gem in the
centre of the town to eat, they go for the Maggie
floorshow. (And they get it anyway whether they
went for it or not!)

Maggie is the owner; she used to run the
Boathouse restaurant on the river with much the
same team and the same powerhouse brand of
front-of-house management. All-singing, all-seeing,
she has a joke and a quip for every customer. You
have been warned.

The food is in the same top gear, both in zippy,
worldwide flavour combos and in speed of
delivery. It may have something to do with serving
up so many pre-theatre suppers but there's no
hanging around here.

It's a place you will warm to. Rustic, pretty and
relaxed, it feels almost seasidey. There are candles
on the bare tables, lots of specials on the
blackboard and music (including some from Maggie).

The tantalising menu offers appealingly modern ideas, such as mackerel fillet with piccalilli and potato cake, spiced confit black leg chicken on tarragon broth, seared sea bass on caramelised cabbage with tomato chilli jam.

Some starters sound more like main courses (pot roast belly pork with basmati and guava for instance) but they pull it off with well-combined and balanced flavours. The wine list is short but has pleasant surprises, such as young, fresh Picpoul from the Languedoc (good with the fish dishes especially). Puds are less surprising but high on comfort value and the coffee is Illy - great taste indeed.

Russons

8 Church Street, Stratford, Warks, CV37 6HB.
01789 268822.

Eclectic

Tues-Sat
11.30-1.45,
5.30-9.45.

CC
(no Diners;
slips closed).
A/C.
4 V.

Starters
£3.50-£6.

Mains
£6.95-£15.

Desserts
£4.25.

One of those traditional tea shop-looking places, Russons keeps its many regulars more than happy with reliably cooked and tasty fare.

Thoroughly respectable it may be but you may still find yourself surprised by the more-than-acceptable cooking, even with the volume of choice available. And it's not all tried-and-tested bangers'n'mash-style, although that's all decent enough.

There are the classics like chicken supreme or grilled sirloin with garlic and herb butter (dishes which never really went away), as well as more brasserie-ish selections like lamb's liver and smoked bacon.

There's the traditional sort of food overload - too much rice and salad with a main course of baked aubergine already loaded with goat's cheese, for instance but its generous heart is the right place. A beamed, pretty place which also dishes up pre-theatre suppers. And you might need a good sit down after a meal here.

The Vintner

4-5 Sheep Street, Stratford, Warks, CV37 6EF.
01789 297259.
Website: www.the-vintner.co.uk

Modern European
Mon-Sat
10.30-10.
Sun
10.30-9.30.
CC
(slips left open).
2 V.
Starters
£1.75-£6.50.
Mains
£8.95-£15.50.
Desserts
£3.95.

A well-known and well-established brasserie in a
wonderfully quirky, 400-year-old building.

Soups are original, large salads are seasonal with a
good house dressing and classics such as fish pie
and lasagne are as good as you'll find anywhere.
The food comes fast but it's still a relaxing place to
linger with friends over your coffee.

Service starts with breakfasts from 10am and goes
through till 10pm with afternoon snacks and pre-
theatre meals all catered for. The menu changes
every couple of months and offers lighter bites
through to full meals with a specials list that often
provides another 10 options. There may be veal
escalope on penne, sirloin steak with dolcelatte
sauce, carpaccio of beef with Harry's Bar salsa
among the choices. A wide range of bottled beers
supplements a wine list that sticks to the classics
and is sensibly priced.

The look is rather Hotel du Vin with wooden
floors, wine artefacts and memorabilia - but
nothing cluttered or prissy.

Staff are young, attentive and knowledgeable;
most are longstanding, a good sign.

STUDLEY

The Indonesian

73 Alcester Road, Studley, Warks, B80 7NJ.
01527 857207.

Indonesian
Every day
6-11.
Wheelchair access.
CC
(no Diners;
slips left open).
A/C.
7 V.

This is one of those restaurants where first
appearances are decidedly deceptive. The
exterior is hardly welcoming and the layout wins it
no friends. The menu, whilst authentic, is not user-
friendly and a little guidance from the owner is
much recommended.

The tastes on offer, however, are something special. A delicate combination of spice and fruit wins rave reviews - one great fan says it's the best Indonesian food he's tasted outside Indonesia (and Amsterdam). The satay starters are marinated and barbecued to perfection. For the main course, the beef rendang is magnificent and, best of all, the vermicelli noodles have a piquancy to sharpen any appetite.

The wine list, though limited, is cheap. The best accompaniment is probably the oriental beer.

Service can be slow if they're busy and Studley being Studley, the neighbouring pizza takeaway is usually why the parking can be awkward.

Starters
£2.95-£5.95.

Mains
£5.95-£8.

Desserts
£2.75.

Set menus
£10, £12.50, £15.

SUTTON COLDFIELD

La Cote d'Or

358 Birmingham Road, Wylde Green,
Sutton Coldfield, B72 1YH.
0121 373 7117.

A refurbished, snug little place in a row of shops on a busy road, La Cote d'Or is owned by a Burgundian who also runs the kitchen.

The food is, therefore, as French as you'd expect (snails may well be available), with numbers of dishes kept to sensibly manageable limits and two good value set menus as well as an à la carte with which to play the mix and match game

Care is taken with ingredients, knowledgeable staff are a real bonus and provincial simplicity is a keynote when it comes to the cuisine. It all works nicely most of the time, as in a starter of a goat's cheese tart blessed with great pastry, sweet caramelised onions and baby spinach or a dessert of strawberries steeped in balsamic vinegar, a great double whammy of sweetness and back-of-the-throat zing, dished up with a creamy sabayon sauce.

Expect rare meat to be as the French understand it and with such classic gallic accompaniments as

French provincial
Tues-Sat
12-2, 7-10.
CC
(slips left open).
Wheelchair access.
A/C.
Free range.
1 V.
Starters
£3.95-£5.95.
Mains
£9.95-£15.95.
Desserts
£3.95-£5.95.
Table d'hote
£16.95 - 3 courses.

beurre café de Paris (herb-laden butter). If the market delivers, there should be some fine fresh fish around too, treated with the respect it deserves.

New Hall Hotel ★

Walmley Road, Sutton Coldfield, B76 1QX.
0121 378 2442. Fax 0121 378 4637.
Website: www.newhallhotel.net

For those who want to push the boat out in credit card-hammering style, this could well be the place.

New Hall is a gorgeous, listed, moated hotel but the food, while consummately stylish and superbly presented, has had its critics, who find it rather insubstantial and too nouvelle cuisine-ish for the considerable amount of money it costs.

Still, a warm salad of roast quail with French beans and a saffron risotto made for tantalising starters while the array of main courses made choosing a pleasantly difficult task. Fish dishes are spot-on fresh, accompaniments - perhaps sarladaise potatoes, pak choi and an excellent green peppercorn sauce with duck - are well-chosen and desserts hit the sweet-toothed spot.

Such ethereal fare adds up to a typical bill for two weighing in at more than £110, not helped by a quality wine list (all the classics plus some braver suggestions from the New World and Israel) which kicks off at £15.

Modern British
Every day
12.30-2, 7-9.30.

CC
(slips left open).
Wheelchair access
(+WC).
3 V.

L and D
£29.50 - 3 courses,

alc
£39.50 - 3 courses,
£33.50 - 2 courses.

Oriel ★

290-292 Lichfield Road, Mere Green,
Sutton Coldfield, B74 2UG.
0121 323 4600. Fax 0121 323 1839.
Website: www.orielrestaurant.co.uk

The owners of Chandlers in Lichfield have branched out with this spacious gem which has got the locals flocking to the suburban shopping

Modern European
Mon-Fri
12-2, 6-10.

Sat
6-10.

Sun
12-3, 6-9.

centre spot previously occupied by Casa Tinos.

It's still Mediterranean-based for food but the decor has changed completely. A circular bar dominates the liner-style ground floor and an elegant stairway to heaven - or the dining room anyway - leads the hungry below decks.

The curved-wall restaurant is airily modern and beautifully contemporary, decked out with fabulous wall decorations made of glass and huge mirrors. Even the loos are a treat.

Anything goes with the menu - English, Spanish, Italian, French, even Thai and Chinese. Vegetarians get plenty of choice too.

No modern ingredient is overlooked, from wasabi and pickled ginger with the seared tuna to tamarind with duck and wild rocket with a sun-dried tomato risotto. Starters could feature crab and lobster cappuccino or kidney turbigo, savoy cabbage with fennel seeds.

Cooking abilities keep up to the mark at main course too with slow-roast belly pork well-matched with Asian spices and bok choi but they can also keep things simple - Dover sole or lobster not requiring too much gilding. Even pizzas make an appearance, should there be any tastes left uncatered for.

CC
(slips left open).
Wheelchair access
(+WC).
5 V.

Starters
£4.25-£5.50.

Mains
£9.50-£14.

Desserts
£4.35-£7.95.

Table d'hote
L
£8.75 - 2 courses,
£12 - 3 courses.

D
£11.75 - 2 courses,
£15 - 3 courses.

Pizza Express

5 Birmingham Road, B72 1QQ.
0121 354 9261.
See Birmingham entry.

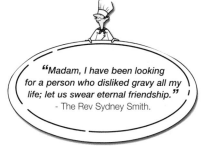

"Madam, I have been looking for a person who disliked gravy all my life; let us swear eternal friendship." - The Rev Sydney Smith.

SWINFEN

Swinfen Hall ★

Swinfen, near Lichfield, Staffs, WS14 9RS.
01543 481494. Fax: 01543 480341.
Email: swinfen.hall@virgin.net

Modern British
Mon-Fri
12.30-2, 7.30-9.

Sat
7.30-9.30

Sun
12.30-2

CC
(slips left open).
Wheelchair access.
Freerange.
2 V.

Starters
£5.50-£8.25.

Mains
£14-£23.50.

Desserts
£4.25-£10.95.

Tactfully ignore the young offenders' institution next door and imagine yourself in some gracious period TV drama as you drive up to this picturebook mansion.

This is grand living on a grand scale - huge rooms with huge windows and huge curtains and huge sofas. The grounds beg admiring glances as you sip your pre-dinner drink.

Despite the obvious formality - all polished furniture, silverware and antiques - the approachable staff are down to earth and there's little of that stuffiness that can cast a deathly pall on some posh dining rooms.

The food's satisfying too, classically based of course, although contemporary touches like bubble and squeak (here with roast quail) also come into their own.

TITLEY

Stagg Inn ★

Titley, Kington, Herefordshire, HR5 3RL.
01544 230221.
Email: reservations@thestagg.co.uk
Website: www.thestagg.co.uk

Modern British
Tues-Sat
12-2, 6.30-10.

Sun
12-2, 7-9.

CC
(no Amex, Diners).
Local/free
range/organic.
2 V.

In the middle of this most rural of counties, the Stagg struck a tremendous national first - the only pub in Britain to be awarded a coveted Michelin star.

It's a great pat on the back for the talented cooking of Roux brothers-trained chef-owner Steve Reynolds, who runs this pubbily down to earth place with partner Nicola Holland. His menus are grounded in the excellent produce of the region - Marches beef, lamb, marvellous cheeses. Meat and poultry is often organic and/or free range.

He follows the seasons too with intelligent dishes that put a spin on tried-and-tested combinations. A pork tenderloin may be stuffed with dried fruits or a fillet of salmon poached in duck fat for extra depth of flavour. Rack of lamb with dauphinoise potatoes and fennel and garlic purée is classically perfect and properly rare.

Vegetarian fare is imaginative and gets plenty of flavour from well-treated vegetables (veggies get their own menu with three or four starters and two or three main courses). A well-chosen wine list offers more than enough variety to keep up with the food standards.

Starters
£3-£6.50.

Mains
£9.90-£14.50.

Desserts
£3.90-£4.90.

Sun L
£11.50 – 3 courses.

ULLINGSWICK

Three Crowns Inn ★

Ullingswick, Herefordshire, HR1 3JQ.
01432 820279.
Email: info@threecrownsinn.demon.co.uk
Website: www.threecrownsinn.demon.co.uk

Down a beautiful country lane, the Three Crowns plies its trade quietly and without fuss. Yet the food on offer here is wonderful and has won it awards for its celebration of excellent local produce.

The menu will depend, and quite rightly too, on what is seasonally available and/or at its best. There could be some excellent wild mushrooms that a fungi-fancying friend has brought in, or something particularly good from the pub's productive garden.

Whatever it is, chef Brent Castle will turn it - without too much tampering - into a delicious dish to be chalked up on the blackboard which dominates one wall in this quaint, hopbine-decorated little pub.

Traditional

Mon/Wed/
Thurs/Fri/Sat
12-2, 7-9.30.

Sun
12-2, 7-9.

CC
(no Amex, Diners;
slips closed).
Wheelchair access.
Local/free
range/organic.
1 V.

Starters
average £4.95.

Mains average
£12.95.

Desserts
£3.95.

There may be roast Marches lamb with sauce bèarnaise, a grilled sirloin of Marches beef with warm herb salsa or perhaps tagliatelle with wild mushrooms, asparagus and brown butter vinaigrette. The dairy quotient can be high so butter and cream fans will be on cloud nine; this is indulgent stuff.

If the weather's fine, do sit outside - not only is it pretty, it's also quiet. Forget taped music or the drone of constant traffic, here you can actually hear the birds sing. A marvellous place - it's just a shame that most of us will have to use our cars to get there.

UPPER SLAUGHTER

Lords of the Manor ★

Upper Slaughter, near Bourton-on-the-Water, Glos, GL54 2JD.
01451 820243. Fax 01451 820696.
Email: lordsofthemanor@btinternet.com

Innovative modern British

Every day 12.30-2, 7-9.30.

CC (slips closed).
Wheelchair access.
3 V.
Organic/free range.

Starters £9.50-£13.

Mains £22-£26.

Desserts £8-£11.

Tasting menu £49 - 7 courses.

You might think looking at this blissful Cotswold mansion that the menu would hold few surprises - a roll call of French classics, staid genteel fare for the big of wallet and unadventurous of taste.

But hold hard - for this luxuriously-elegant restaurant provides more culinary gobsmacking moments per square foot than anywhere else north of the Fat Duck at Bray.

It's the ice creams that do it (there's a particularly excellent ice cream machine on the market that must be going to chefs' heads). Perhaps avocado ice cream with crab risotto? What about onion ice cream with slow-cooked beef fillet? Mustard sherbert as a between-course palate-cleanser anyone? Bacon ice cream with your pineapple soufflé?

Even without the ice cream, there's little letting up on the mixing and matching - smoked eel macaroni accompany salmon mi-cuit, for instance. Elsewhere, the flavours are based on tried-and tested flavour combinations although in unusual forms - a vanilla hollandaise with sea bass, mustard tortellini with tournedos of rabbit.

For the most part, these staggering leaps of imagination, although very challenging, work astoundingly well, revealing a chef of sharp intelligence as well as inspired creativity.

Flavours are concentrated and vibrantly clear; technique is beyond question, presentation superb. There's no fear of strange body parts - as a starter of pickled lamb tongues with John Dory testifies. There is also a generous amount of what Egon Ronay calls 'force-feeding' - those pre- and mid-course snacks so you don't get restless.

Serious gourmet territory like this is worth saving up for. When so many meals out are so similar, Lords of the Manor is splendidly different. The white-water-rafting alternative to so much package holiday dullness.

WARWICK

Findons ★

7 Old Square, Warwick CV34 4RA.
01926 411755. Fax: 01926 400453.
Website: www.findons-restaurant.co.uk

Modern British

Mon-Fri
12-2, 7-9.30.

Sat
7-9.30.

1 V.
CC
(slips left open).
A/C.
Wheelchair access.
Free range/organic.

Starters
£3.95-£9.95.

Mains
£10.95-£18.95.

Desserts
£5.95-£7.95.

Set menus available.

Chef-patron Michael Findon's eponymous restaurant is in a superb 18th century townhouse tucked away in a splendid square by the church in the centre of this lovely town. A picture postcard scene if ever there was.

The elegance is unmistakeable but there's no stiff upper lip. The music of Miles Davis set a laidback tone during one visit while the pictures, panelling and books create the feel of a real house (albeit a classy one) rather than a soulless restaurant. Fine dining but all relaxed class, mellow and friendly. A genuine, comfortable ambience.

The cooking is modern in outlook but solidly grounded in technique and labour intensiveness.

A lot of care goes on here and it's clear both in presentation and the scope of the menu. But there is also enough confidence to keep things simple.

A pavé of salmon with avocado and watercress is a statement of classic restraint while flair sparkles in the pairing of black cherries, honey and rum with duck breast. Orange and oregano become partners for sea bass while baby chard, rocket and a timbale of butternut squash give king scallops masses of taste. Quality and the striving for it is clear throughout. Findons is one of those immensely comfortable places which knows where it's at, knows what it does well and happily does them to a T.

Robbies

74 Smith Street, Warwick. CV34 4HU.
01926 400470.

Modern British.

Tues-Sat
7-late.

CC
(no Amex, Diners;
slips left open).
Local produce.
4 V.

Starters
£3.70-£5.50.

Mains
£12.50-£15.50.

Desserts
£3-£4.50.

Small, laidback and friendly, Robbies has a useful role to play in Warwick's restaurant life - it feels pleasantly like a neighbourhood eaterie but it's in the middle of town and it aims high with its menu.

The mateyness is almost devil-may-care and youthful but the smooth mix of old jazz classics in the background crosses any generation gaps with quiet taste. It feels more like a friends' meeting place (and I'm not talking Quakers but funnily enough, it isn't licensed although you can bring your own.) The small interior has nice touches, like the stained glass round the front door.

Flavours are also pretty up to date and lively combinations keep everyone wide awake, from a spicy guacamole with chickpea and lentil fritters to a honey and ginger wine sauce with pan-seared fillet steak. It's hale and hearty, with plenty of choice for carnivores and herbivores alike. Puds like homemade chocolate and blackberry ice cream with fresh baked cookies can be a particular comfort zone hit.

"Hunger is the best sauce in the world."
- Miguel de Cervantes.

WINCHCOMBE

Wesley House ★

High Street, Winchcombe, Glos. GL54 5LJ.
01242 602366. Fax 01242 609046.
Email: enquiries@wesleyhouse.co.uk
Website: www.wesleyhouse.co.uk

Just round the corner from Sudeley Castle is this charming 15th century building on the chintzy town's high street (it's not actually a manor house - it just sounds like one).

A small bar and seating area (by a big log fire) leads through to a pretty if traditional dining room where a spiral staircase exists solely as a display case for a collection of jelly moulds and other aesthetically pleasing pottery bits.

The accent is on the feminine elsewhere too, with roses in wine glasses of water echoing a view of a pretty balcony and garden beyond.

Cooking is sound and generous with the emphasis on generosity and variety. As well as à la carte and set menus, there are various specials to choose from too.

Salads are tasty and fill the generous plates while ingredients such as fish and quality beef get a simple treatment which gives flavours full rein. Not that this lack of frilliness means ignoring details - there may be a sunblush tomato dressing with a tart of roast courgette and the artisan West Country cheese Cornish Yarg while green beans may come bacon-wrapped.

There's a feeling of real freshness with this straightforward approach and there are major treats to look forward to when it comes to the dessert course - maybe a chocolate 'tear drop' with chocolate sauce or 'double peach' ice cream adding luxury to a fresh fruit gratin or - best of all - a grillotine cherry crème brulèe, a real stunner.

Modern British

Mon-Sat
12-2, 6.45-9.

Sun
12-2.

CC
(slips left open).
Wheelchair access.
Local/organic
produce.
1 V.

L
£10 - 2 courses,
£14.50 - 3 courses.

Early bird menu
(Mon-Fri
6.45-7.45)
£18.50/£21.50.

D
£26 - 2 courses,
£31 - 3 courses.

WISHAW

The De Vere Belfry ★

The French Restaurant, Wishaw,
north Warwickshire, B76 9PR.
01675 470301. Fax 01675 470178.
E-mail: enquiries@thebelfry.com.
Website: www.devereonline.co.uk

Modern British
and French

Sun-Fri
12.30-2.30,
7.30-10.

Sat
7.30-10.

CC.
Wheelchair access
(+WC).
A/C.
3 V.

Starters
£2-£7.

Mains
£6-£15.

Desserts
£3-£7.

Set menus also
available.

It's a thought which either gladdens your heart or makes your toes curl - a roomful of golfers in scarlet Slazenger sweaters and checked slacks.

But never fear. Diners in the French restaurant at this enormous sporting mecca ditch the nightmare fashion kit and appear like normal people (at least, there wasn't a single Pringle on the night I was there).

The restaurant has some good staff and the food knows its niche. We're in the corporate world here so we're talking expensive of course and aware of its social standing. If silver domes are your thing, this is the place for you.

There'll be quality olives to nibble and appetisers - perhaps a teeny risotto with chorizo - before the main French-based choices follow. The food is generally good, if not always up to its price tag (the wine list is expensive too). The traditional big hitters - chateaubriand of Scotch fillet, roast venison - are often the big successes, teamed imaginatively, in the venison's case, with haggis and whisky cream.

"Many's the night I've dreamt of cheese, toasted mostly."
- Ben Gunn, Treasure Island.
(Robert Louis Stevenson)

WOLVERHAMPTON

Bilash Tandoori ★★

2 Cheapside, Wolverhampton. WV1 1TU.
01902 427762. Fax: 01902 311991.
Email: enquiries@bilash-tandoori.co.uk
Website: www.bilash-tandoori.co.uk

Bangladeshi

Mon-Sat
12-2.30, 6-11.30.

Mon
6-11.30.

CC
(slips left open).
Wheelchair access.
A/C.
7+ V.

Starters
£3.90-£5.90.

Mains
£8.90-£18.90.

Desserts
£3.95.

Set L
£7.50.

Set banquet
£21.90.

When it comes to Bilash, I'm a bit of a bore. I sing its praises to all and sundry because I believe it leaves all other Indian restaurants standing.

The only pain factor involved in a Bilash trip is the (for me) long drive to Wolverhampton. (Others visit regularly from as far afield as the Cotswolds). Negotiating the nightmare ring road system (follow the signs to the Civic Centre - it's right next door) is the next hurdle. Then, it's all plain sailing into the comfort zone.

Bilash looks like a suburban Indian restaurant (it's actually Bangladeshi but forgive my use of the convenient label) but its food is something else and has won chef-patron Sitab Khan many accolades.

There is real passion here, enormous commitment and equally enormous amounts of hard labour, happily done. They grind and mix their own spices and many of the excellent ingredients - fresh curry leaves, huge prawns, fresh mangoes to name but three - are specially imported by another branch of the family.

Sitab's son Mohammed is in charge of service and more than happy (unstoppable even) to talk about the food - how the rice is steamed, not boiled, with saffron and cardamom, how they make their own jammily-delicious mango chutney, how they use olive or sunflower oil instead of heavy ghee to make the dishes lighter.

But the proof is in tasting it for yourself - try the deceptively simple but superb tandoor-cooked chicken chaat, followed by an exquisite Goan tiger prawn massala, maybe. Vegetarians get an excellent choice, with a wonderfully fragrant niramish or deliciously savoury kofta dumplings among some of my personal highlights.

Prices are higher than run-of-the-mill places but justifiably so. You may prefer the Indian beer as an accompaniment rather than wine.

WORCESTER

Browns ★

24 Quay Street, Worcester. WR1 2JJ.
01905 26263. Fax 01905 25768.

Modern British
Tues-Fri
12.30-1.45;
7.30-9.30.

Sat
7.30-9.30.

Sun
12.30-1.45.

CC
(no Amex;
slips left open).
Wheelchair access
(+WC).
Organic/free
range. 1 V.

L
£19.50 - 3 courses.

D
£36.50 - 3 courses
+ cheese

The riverside location here is one of Brown's great attractions - although a bit close for comfort during the floods.

The building is a stunner too and reeks of classy, serene other-worldliness - and money, in an understated sort of way, of course. This is not a cheap restaurant - £36.50 for three courses, cheese and coffee at dinner puts it in the country house hotel bracket of wallet-lightening.

The converted corn mill has elegant, tall brick walls and beautiful, greenery-framed windows looking out on to the swan-jammed Severn. Get a table here if you can.

Much of the food is basically quality British with international, especially gallic, twists - the beef may perhaps have an oriental flavour, particularly as a starter, while roast duck is served with a confit leg and baked cod has a herb crust.

The wine list is mainly French, good quality and marked up as expected.

This is a lovely place but the bill may leave you expecting more.

Saffrons bistro

15 New Street, Worcester, WR1 2DP.
01905 610505.

Mediterranean/
modern British.

Mon-Thurs
12-2, 6-10.

Fri
12-2, 6-10.30.

Bang in the centre of town but decidedly quaint, Saffrons, a friendly, yellow place, does a good range of bistro classics very well and to a thoroughly appreciative audience.

Starters may go Med - crispy artichoke salad with olives, rocket, parmesan and sun-dried toms, or maybe east with wok-fried Thai salmon served with tzatziki (they're not afraid to create their own fusion specials).

Mains follow very similar routes, with perhaps a beef stroganoff thrown in for good measure or a chunky chargrilled fillet steak topped with stilton to show they can do hearty British too. Flavours are richly satisfying and prices very reasonable.

Sat
12-2.30,
6-10.30.

Sun
12-2.30, 6-10.

CC
(slips left open).
Wheelchair access.
A/C.
3 V.

Starters
£2.75-£6.25.

Mains
£10.75-£15.75.

Desserts
£3.50-£4.50.

Set menus
on request.

WORFIELD

The Old Vicarage ★

Worfield, near Bridgnorth,
Shropshire, WV15 5JZ.
01746 716497. Fax 01746 716552.
Website: www.oldvicarageworfield.com

There are new(ish) owners at this thoroughly decent, stolidly redbrick hotel and restaurant in rural Shropshire but the kitchen brigade, according to latest reports, has stayed mostly the same.

This is archetypal country house hotel land. Pre-dinner drinks can be sipped in the pretty conservatory overlooking the croquet lawn or in the plushly-seated little bar. The menu for the pleasant, traditional dining room shows that food is taken pretty seriously.

This is a highly-polished place - from the wooden floor to the gracious tables as well as the offerings on the menu. Settle into the tasteful blue chairs and maybe indulge yourself with the gourmet menu which features starters such as king scallops with black pudding cake or smoked salmon and crayfish rillettes dressed with Sevruga caviar. Then sample main courses such as fillet of local longhorn beef with foie gras butter sauce or rump of lamb (local again, of course) with mustard mash. Aspirational and a special occasion treat.

Modern British

Mon-Fri
12-2.30, 7-9.

Sat
7-9.

Sun
12-2.30, 7-9.

CC
(slips left open).
Wheelchair access
(+WC).
Free range/organic.
4 V.

L
3 courses - £18.50.

Price for
3-course D
based on main
course choice,
£23-£36.

INDEX